SEEKING
Scripture

ONE YEAR

This journal belongs to:

_____

If found, please contact:

_____

1st Edition, 2024
Hardback ISBN 979-8-9919225-2-4
Paperback ISBN 979-8-9919225-3-1

Table of contents

Forward 4

Tips for Success 5

How to Use this Journal 6

Daily Pages 8

Additional Notes Pages 373

Learn about Seeking Scripture 399

Reading Checklist for Each Book 400

Foreward

I live in anticipation of the day our Messiah returns. I look forward to being united with my brethren in His eternal kingdom, serving one another out of love, and worshiping Him together. I eagerly await a time when the world will be at peace and we will no longer need to teach others about the Father because everyone will know Him, from least to greatest (Jeremiah 31:34).

Until that time comes, I am so grateful for the wonderful community the Father has given us through Seeking Scripture. In this community, I have tasted a wondrous glimpse of what this future with Messiah will be like. Regrettably, it is a rarity in our time for a diverse group of believers to live in harmony with one another...but when you know God, anything is possible! By His gracious hand, we have formed a loving community of believers from all walks of the Christian faith, seemingly every denomination under the sun. Together, we encourage one another as we deepen our faith by growing in knowledge and understanding of the whole Bible.

Whether you have been with us for years or if this book is our first introduction, it is an honor to study our Father's Word alongside you. Our singular goal is to help you read the whole Bible for yourself. In doing so, we know you will be drawn closer to the Father, developing that first hand relationship with Him that we all long for and need, both in this life and through eternity.

To learn more about Seeking Scripture, check out our charter statements found at the end of this book or visit us at SeekingScripture.com.

Together, may we bring further honor and glory to His name.

Sincerely,

Christy Jordan

SEEKING 🏺 SCRIPTURE

Tips For Success

1. Choose a Bible translation that works for you.
The BEST translation is one you will read. Check out
Biblegateway.com or Biblehub.com to read several
translations of a single verse and see which makes more
sense to you.

2. Consider large print.
No matter your age, Bible print is tiny! Large print is much
easier to read and can make time in the Word far more
enjoyable.

3.Keep Reading!
Dedicate yourself to reading daily, but if you miss a few days,
don't berate yourself. Self condemnation can easily bring
your Bible reading to a standstill. Instead, show yourself
grace (It happens to all of us!) and just dive right back in. If
you are reading along with the group, begin right where we
are; you can pick up what you missed in the next reading
cycle. After all, the goal is not to just read the Bible once but
to become daily Bible readers.

4. Choose a time that works best for you.
Some prefer to read first thing in the morning, others find
they retain more if they read in the evenings. Choose the
time that works best for you and do not feel like you are
falling short if you find your best reading times differ from
others.

5. Make God a priority.
Each day, we make time for the things that are important to
us: television shows, Facebook, nightly news, etc. The Creator
of the Universe deserves a spot at the top of that list. I want
to encourage you to make a date with God each day *and don't
stand Him up!*

6. GET EXCITED!
If you've found the Word of God to be dry and impersonal in
the past, get ready for all of that to change. We are going to
begin at the beginning and experience the Word coming to
LIFE like never before and give life to these dry bones!
God's Word is ALIVE, get ready to feel it!

How to use this journal

It is my hope that this journal will become one you want to visit daily, thereby helping you develop and maintain a consistent pattern of daily Bible reading.

Each day contains reading assignments accompanied by a QR code that will take you to my notes for that day's readings. My sincere hope is not that you will always agree with my conclusions, but that through my notes you will learn how to study the Bible for yourself, dig deeper, and test everything to the straight edge of His word.

Use the **notes and reflections section** to make short notes of what stood out to you, list questions for which you hope to find answers, or topics you'd like to dig deeper on.

Also included in each page is a **verse of the day** from each day's readings, with a box to write it out if you would like. If you've never set aside daily time to write out Scripture, you may find it both comforting and satisfying. If you prefer not to, this box can be used to list cross references, to-do lists for the day, or in whatever manner is most useful to you.

Utilize the **weather check boxes** to keep a record of your current environment or get creative and use them to indicate the state of your heart as you read that day.

A **gratitude box** will help you develop a grateful mindset as you continually consider new things to be thankful for.

Each day's **prayer box** can be used to note requests, answered prayers, and ways in which you are placing our hope in the Father for His will and guidance in your life.

And lastly, don't be hesitant about filling in the pages however you wish. Make mistakes and scratch them out or erase them if you like. Write in the margins, ignore the lines if you'd like, and utilize this book as a primary tool while you study the Word.

With just a few minutes each day, this journal will become a treasured keepsake of a year in the life of a maturing believer and a precious time capsule of the relationship between a child and their heavenly Father.

This is what YHWH says:
"Stand at the crossroads and look; ask
for the ancient paths, ask where the
good way is, and walk in it, and you will
find rest for your souls."

Jeremiah 6:16

"I, YHWH, do not change."

Malachi 3:6

Who is YHWH?

SEEKING  SCRIPTURE

DAY 1

Genesis 1-3

NOTES AND REFLECTIONS

Study Notes

_____
_____
_____
_____
_____
_____
_____
_____
_____
_____
_____
_____

VERSE OF THE DAY GENESIS 2:7

TODAY I'M GRATEFUL FOR

1.

2.

3.

PRAYER & PRAISE

SEEKING  SCRIPTURE

NOTES AND REFLECTIONS

Study Notes

VERSE OF THE DAY GENESIS 5:2

PRAYER & PRAISE

TODAY I'M GRATEFUL FOR

1.

2.

3.

SEEKING  SCRIPTURE

DAY 3

Genesis 8-11

NOTES AND REFLECTIONS

Study Notes

_____
_____
_____
_____
_____

_____
_____
_____
_____
_____
_____
_____

VERSE OF THE DAY GENESIS 9:16

PRAYER & PRAISE

TODAY I'M GRATEFUL FOR

1.

2.

3.

SEEKING  SCRIPTURE

NOTES AND REFLECTIONS

Study Notes

VERSE OF THE DAY GENESIS 15:5

PRAYER & PRAISE

TODAY I'M GRATEFUL FOR

1.

2.

3.

DAY 5

Genesis 16-18

NOTES AND REFLECTIONS

Study Notes

VERSE OF THE DAY GENESIS 18:14

PRAYER & PRAISE

TODAY I'M GRATEFUL FOR

1.

2.

3.

SEEKING ✦ SCRIPTURE

NOTES AND REFLECTIONS

Study Notes

_____
_____
_____
_____
_____
_____
_____
_____
_____
_____
_____

VERSE OF THE DAY GENESIS 21:33

PRAYER & PRAISE

TODAY I'M GRATEFUL FOR

1.

2.

3.

SEEKING  SCRIPTURE

DAY 7

Genesis 22-24

NOTES AND REFLECTIONS

Study Notes

_____

VERSE OF THE DAY GENESIS 22:14

PRAYER & PRAISE

TODAY I'M GRATEFUL FOR

1.

2.

3.

SEEKING  SCRIPTURE

NOTES AND REFLECTIONS

Study Notes

VERSE OF THE DAY GENESIS 26:24

PRAYER & PRAISE

TODAY I'M GRATEFUL FOR

1.

2.

3.

SEEKING  SCRIPTURE

DAY 9

Genesis 27-29

NOTES AND REFLECTIONS

Study Notes

VERSE OF THE DAY GENESIS 28:17

PRAYER & PRAISE

TODAY I'M GRATEFUL FOR

1.

2.

3.

SEEKING  SCRIPTURE

NOTES AND REFLECTIONS

Study Notes

VERSE OF THE DAY GENESIS 31:3

PRAYER & PRAISE

TODAY I'M GRATEFUL FOR

1.

2.

3.

DAY 11

Genesis 32-34

NOTES AND REFLECTIONS

Study Notes

VERSE OF THE DAY GENESIS 32:28

PRAYER & PRAISE

TODAY I'M GRATEFUL FOR

1.

2.

3.

SEEKING  SCRIPTURE

NOTES AND REFLECTIONS

Study Notes

VERSE OF THE DAY GENESIS 35:12

PRAYER & PRAISE

TODAY I'M GRATEFUL FOR

1.

2.

3.

SEEKING SCRIPTURE

DAY 13

Genesis 38-40

NOTES AND REFLECTIONS

Study Notes

_____

VERSE OF THE DAY GENESIS 39:3

PRAYER & PRAISE

TODAY I'M GRATEFUL FOR

1.

2.

3.

SEEKING  SCRIPTURE

NOTES AND REFLECTIONS

_____
_____
_____
_____
_____

Study Notes

_____
_____
_____
_____
_____
_____
_____

VERSE OF THE DAY GENESIS 41:38

PRAYER & PRAISE

TODAY I'M GRATEFUL FOR

1.

2.

3.

DAY 15

Genesis 43-45

NOTES AND REFLECTIONS

Study Notes

VERSE OF THE DAY GENESIS 45:5

PRAYER & PRAISE

TODAY I'M GRATEFUL FOR

1.

2.

3.

SEEKING  SCRIPTURE

NOTES AND REFLECTIONS

Study Notes

VERSE OF THE DAY GENESIS 46:27

PRAYER & PRAISE

TODAY I'M GRATEFUL FOR

1.

2.

3.

SEEKING  SCRIPTURE

DAY 17

Genesis 48-50

NOTES AND REFLECTIONS

Study Notes

_____

VERSE OF THE DAY GENESIS 50:25

PRAYER & PRAISE

TODAY I'M GRATEFUL FOR

1.

2.

3.

SEEKING  SCRIPTURE

NOTES AND REFLECTIONS

_____
_____
_____
_____
_____

Study Notes

_____
_____
_____
_____
_____
_____

VERSE OF THE DAY EXODUS 3:15

PRAYER & PRAISE

TODAY I'M GRATEFUL FOR

1.

2.

3.

SEEKING  SCRIPTURE

DAY 19

Exodus 4-6

Study Notes

NOTES AND REFLECTIONS

_____
_____
_____
_____
_____
_____
_____
_____
_____
_____
_____
_____

VERSE OF THE DAY EXODUS 6:7

TODAY I'M GRATEFUL FOR

1.

2.

3.

PRAYER & PRAISE

SEEKING  SCRIPTURE

NOTES AND REFLECTIONS

_____

_____

_____

_____

_____

Study Notes

_____

_____

_____

_____

_____

_____

VERSE OF THE DAY EXODUS 9:20-21

PRAYER & PRAISE

☀ ⛅ ☁ 🌧 ⛈ ❄
☐ ☐ ☐ ☐ ☐ ☐

TODAY I'M GRATEFUL FOR

1.

2.

3.

SEEKING  SCRIPTURE

DAY 21

Exodus 10-12

NOTES AND REFLECTIONS

Study Notes

_____
_____
_____
_____
_____
_____
_____
_____
_____
_____
_____
_____

VERSE OF THE DAY EXODUS 12:12

TODAY I'M GRATEFUL FOR

1.

2.

3.

PRAYER & PRAISE

SEEKING  SCRIPTURE

NOTES AND REFLECTIONS

Study Notes

VERSE OF THE DAY EXODUS 15:11

PRAYER & PRAISE

TODAY I'M GRATEFUL FOR

1.

2.

3.

SEEKING  SCRIPTURE

DAY 23

Exodus 16-18

NOTES AND REFLECTIONS

Study Notes

VERSE OF THE DAY EXODUS 16:27

PRAYER & PRAISE

TODAY I'M GRATEFUL FOR

1.

2.

3.

SEEKING  SCRIPTURE

NOTES AND REFLECTIONS

Exodus 19-21

Study Notes

_____

VERSE OF THE DAY EXODUS 20:20

PRAYER & PRAISE

☀ ⛅ ☁ 🌧 ⛈ ❄
☐ ☐ ☐ ☐ ☐ ☐

TODAY I'M GRATEFUL FOR

1.

2.

3.

SEEKING  SCRIPTURE

DAY 25

Exodus 22-24

Study Notes

VERSE OF THE DAY EXODUS 24:12

PRAYER & PRAISE

TODAY I'M GRATEFUL FOR

1.

2.

3.

SEEKING  SCRIPTURE

NOTES AND REFLECTIONS

Exodus 25-27

Study Notes

VERSE OF THE DAY EXODUS 25:2

PRAYER & PRAISE

TODAY I'M GRATEFUL FOR

1.

2.

3.

SEEKING SCRIPTURE

DAY 27

Exodus 28-29

Study Notes

VERSE OF THE DAY EXODUS 28:36

PRAYER & PRAISE

TODAY I'M GRATEFUL FOR

1.

2.

3.

SEEKING  SCRIPTURE

Exodus 30-32

NOTES AND REFLECTIONS

Study Notes

VERSE OF THE DAY EXODUS 33:19

PRAYER & PRAISE

TODAY I'M GRATEFUL FOR

1.

2.

3.

SEEKING  SCRIPTURE

DAY 29

Exodus 33-35

NOTES AND REFLECTIONS

Study Notes

_____
_____
_____
_____
_____
_____
_____
_____
_____
_____
_____

VERSE OF THE DAY EXODUS 34:6

PRAYER & PRAISE

TODAY I'M GRATEFUL FOR

1.

2.

3.

SEEKING  SCRIPTURE

NOTES AND REFLECTIONS

Study Notes

VERSE OF THE DAY EXODUS 36:2

PRAYER & PRAISE

TODAY I'M GRATEFUL FOR

1.

2.

3.

SEEKING  SCRIPTURE

DAY 31

Exodus 39-40

NOTES AND REFLECTIONS

Study Notes

VERSE OF THE DAY EXODUS 40:16-17

PRAYER & PRAISE

TODAY I'M GRATEFUL FOR

1.

2.

3.

DAY 32

NOTES AND REFLECTIONS

Leviticus 1-4

Study Notes

_____
_____
_____
_____
_____
_____
_____
_____
_____
_____
_____
_____

VERSE OF THE DAY LEVITICUS 2:3

PRAYER & PRAISE

TODAY I'M GRATEFUL FOR

1.

2.

3.

SEEKING  SCRIPTURE

DAY 33

Leviticus 5-7

NOTES AND REFLECTIONS

Study Notes

_____

VERSE OF THE DAY LEVITICUS 7:16

PRAYER & PRAISE

TODAY I'M GRATEFUL FOR

1.

2.

3.

SEEKING  SCRIPTURE

NOTES AND REFLECTIONS

Study Notes

VERSE OF THE DAY LEVITICUS 10:3

PRAYER & PRAISE

TODAY I'M GRATEFUL FOR

1.

2.

3.

SEEKING  SCRIPTURE

DAY 35

Leviticus 11-13

NOTES AND REFLECTIONS

Study Notes

_____

VERSE OF THE DAY LEVITICUS 11:44

PRAYER & PRAISE

TODAY I'M GRATEFUL FOR

1.

2.

3.

SEEKING  SCRIPTURE

NOTES AND REFLECTIONS

Study Notes

VERSE OF THE DAY LEVITICUS 15:31

PRAYER & PRAISE

TODAY I'M GRATEFUL FOR

1.

2.

3.

SEEKING  SCRIPTURE

DAY 37

Leviticus 16-18

NOTES AND REFLECTIONS

Study Notes

_____

_____

_____

_____

_____

_____

_____

_____

_____

_____

_____

VERSE OF THE DAY LEVITICUS 18:4-5

PRAYER & PRAISE

TODAY I'M GRATEFUL FOR

1.

2.

3.

SEEKING  SCRIPTURE

NOTES AND REFLECTIONS

Leviticus 19-21

Study Notes

VERSE OF THE DAY LEVITICUS 19:2

PRAYER & PRAISE

TODAY I'M GRATEFUL FOR

1.

2.

3.

SEEKING  SCRIPTURE

DAY 39

Leviticus 22-23

NOTES AND REFLECTIONS

Study Notes

_____

_____

_____

_____

_____

_____

_____

_____

_____

_____

_____

_____

VERSE OF THE DAY LEVITICUS 23:2

PRAYER & PRAISE

TODAY I'M GRATEFUL FOR

1.

2.

3.

SEEKING SCRIPTURE

NOTES AND REFLECTIONS

Leviticus 24-25

Study Notes

VERSE OF THE DAY LEVITICUS 24:22

PRAYER & PRAISE

TODAY I'M GRATEFUL FOR

1.

2.

3.

SEEKING  SCRIPTURE

DAY 41

Leviticus 26-27

Study Notes

NOTES AND REFLECTIONS

_____
_____
_____
_____
_____

_____
_____
_____
_____
_____
_____

VERSE OF THE DAY LEVITICUS 26:2

PRAYER & PRAISE

TODAY I'M GRATEFUL FOR

1.

2.

3.

SEEKING  SCRIPTURE

DAY 42

Numbers 1-2

NOTES AND REFLECTIONS

_____
_____
_____
_____
_____

Study Notes

_____
_____
_____
_____
_____
_____
_____
_____

VERSE OF THE DAY NUMBERS 1:54

_____
_____
_____
_____
_____
_____
_____

PRAYER & PRAISE

TODAY I'M GRATEFUL FOR

1.

2.

3.

SEEKING  SCRIPTURE

DAY 43

Numbers 3-4

Study Notes

NOTES AND REFLECTIONS

VERSE OF THE DAY NUMBERS 4:49

PRAYER & PRAISE

TODAY I'M GRATEFUL FOR

1.

2.

3.

SEEKING  SCRIPTURE

NOTES AND REFLECTIONS

Study Notes

VERSE OF THE DAY NUMBERS 6:24-26

PRAYER & PRAISE

TODAY I'M GRATEFUL FOR

1.

2.

3.

SEEKING  SCRIPTURE

DAY 45

Numbers 7

Study Notes

VERSE OF THE DAY NUMBERS 7:89

PRAYER & PRAISE

TODAY I'M GRATEFUL FOR

1.

2.

3.

SEEKING  SCRIPTURE

NOTES AND REFLECTIONS

Study Notes

VERSE OF THE DAY NUMBERS 9:14

PRAYER & PRAISE

TODAY I'M GRATEFUL FOR

1.

2.

3.

DAY 47

Numbers 11-13

Study Notes

NOTES AND REFLECTIONS

VERSE OF THE DAY NUMBERS 12:3

PRAYER & PRAISE

TODAY I'M GRATEFUL FOR

1.

2.

3.

SEEKING  SCRIPTURE

NOTES AND REFLECTIONS

Study Notes

VERSE OF THE DAY NUMBERS 15:39

PRAYER & PRAISE

TODAY I'M GRATEFUL FOR

1.

2.

3.

SEEKING  SCRIPTURE

DAY 49

Numbers 16-17

NOTES AND REFLECTIONS

Study Notes

VERSE OF THE DAY NUMBERS 17:10

PRAYER & PRAISE

TODAY I'M GRATEFUL FOR

1.

2.

3.

SEEKING  SCRIPTURE

NOTES AND REFLECTIONS

Numbers 18-20

Study Notes

VERSE OF THE DAY NUMBERS 18:6

PRAYER & PRAISE

TODAY I'M GRATEFUL FOR

1.

2.

3.

SEEKING  SCRIPTURE

DAY 51

Numbers 21-22

Study Notes

VERSE OF THE DAY NUMBERS 21:16

PRAYER & PRAISE

TODAY I'M GRATEFUL FOR

1.

2.

3.

SEEKING  SCRIPTURE

NOTES AND REFLECTIONS

Numbers 23-25

Study Notes

VERSE OF THE DAY NUMBERS 23:19

PRAYER & PRAISE

TODAY I'M GRATEFUL FOR

1.

2.

3.

SEEKING  SCRIPTURE

DAY 53

Numbers 26-27

Study Notes

NOTES AND REFLECTIONS

VERSE OF THE DAY NUMBERS 27:12

PRAYER & PRAISE

TODAY I'M GRATEFUL FOR

1.

2.

3.

SEEKING  SCRIPTURE

NOTES AND REFLECTIONS

Study Notes

VERSE OF THE DAY NUMBERS 28:2

PRAYER & PRAISE

TODAY I'M GRATEFUL FOR

1.

2.

3.

SEEKING SCRIPTURE

DAY 55

Numbers 31-32

NOTES AND REFLECTIONS

Study Notes

_____

VERSE OF THE DAY NUMBERS 32:13

PRAYER & PRAISE

TODAY I'M GRATEFUL FOR

1.

2.

3.

SEEKING  SCRIPTURE

NOTES AND REFLECTIONS

Numbers 33-34

Study Notes

_____
_____
_____
_____
_____
_____
_____
_____
_____
_____
_____
_____
_____
_____

VERSE OF THE DAY NUMBERS 33:55

PRAYER & PRAISE

TODAY I'M GRATEFUL FOR

1.

2.

3.

DAY 57

Numbers 35-36

Study Notes

NOTES AND REFLECTIONS

VERSE OF THE DAY NUMBERS 35:2

PRAYER & PRAISE

TODAY I'M GRATEFUL FOR

1.

2.

3.

SEEKING SCRIPTURE

NOTES AND REFLECTIONS

Deuteronomy 1-2

_____
_____
_____
_____
_____

Study Notes

_____
_____
_____
_____
_____
_____

VERSE OF THE DAY DEUTERONOMY 2:7

_____
_____
_____
_____
_____
_____
_____

PRAYER & PRAISE

TODAY I'M GRATEFUL FOR

1.

2.

3.

SEEKING  SCRIPTURE

DAY 59

Deuteronomy 3-4

Study Notes

NOTES AND REFLECTIONS

_____
_____
_____
_____
_____
_____
_____
_____
_____
_____
_____

VERSE OF THE DAY DEUTERONOMY 4:39

TODAY I'M GRATEFUL FOR

1.

2.

3.

PRAYER & PRAISE

SEEKING  SCRIPTURE

NOTES AND REFLECTIONS

Deuteronomy 5-7

Study Notes

VERSE OF THE DAY DEUTERONOMY 6:4-6

PRAYER & PRAISE

TODAY I'M GRATEFUL FOR

1.

2.

3.

DAY 61

Deuteronomy 8-10

NOTES AND REFLECTIONS

Study Notes

VERSE OF THE DAY DEUTERONOMY 8:6

PRAYER & PRAISE

TODAY I'M GRATEFUL FOR

1.

2.

3.

SEEKING  SCRIPTURE

NOTES AND REFLECTIONS

Study Notes

_____

VERSE OF THE DAY DEUTERONOMY 13:3

PRAYER & PRAISE

TODAY I'M GRATEFUL FOR

1.

2.

3.

SEEKING  SCRIPTURE

DAY 63

Deuteronomy 14-16

NOTES AND REFLECTIONS

Study Notes

_____

_____

_____

_____

_____

_____

_____

_____

_____

_____

_____

VERSE OF THE DAY DEUTERONOMY 14:2

PRAYER & PRAISE

TODAY I'M GRATEFUL FOR

1.

2.

3.

SEEKING  SCRIPTURE

NOTES AND REFLECTIONS

Deuteronomy 17-20

Study Notes

_____
_____
_____
_____
_____
_____
_____
_____
_____
_____
_____
_____

VERSE OF THE DAY DEUTERONOMY 18:2

PRAYER & PRAISE

☀ ⛅ ☁ 🌧 ⛈ ❄
☐ ☐ ☐ ☐ ☐ ☐

TODAY I'M GRATEFUL FOR

1.

2.

3.

DAY 65

Deuteronomy 21-23

NOTES AND REFLECTIONS

Study Notes

VERSE OF THE DAY DEUTERONOMY 21:8

PRAYER & PRAISE

TODAY I'M GRATEFUL FOR

1.

2.

3.

SEEKING  SCRIPTURE

NOTES AND REFLECTIONS

Deuteronomy 24-27

Study Notes

_____

_____

_____

_____

_____

_____

_____

_____

_____

_____

_____

_____

VERSE OF THE DAY DEUTERONOMY 24:19

PRAYER & PRAISE

TODAY I'M GRATEFUL FOR

1.

2.

3.

SEEKING  SCRIPTURE

DAY 67

Deuteronomy 28-29

Study Notes

NOTES AND REFLECTIONS

_____
_____
_____
_____
_____
_____
_____
_____
_____
_____
_____

VERSE OF THE DAY DEUTERONOMY 29:29

PRAYER & PRAISE

TODAY I'M GRATEFUL FOR

1.

2.

3.

SEEKING  SCRIPTURE

NOTES AND REFLECTIONS

Deuteronomy 30-31

Study Notes

_____
_____
_____
_____
_____
_____
_____
_____
_____
_____
_____
_____

VERSE OF THE DAY DEUTERONOMY 30:11

PRAYER & PRAISE

TODAY I'M GRATEFUL FOR

1.

2.

3.

SEEKING  SCRIPTURE

DAY 69

Deuteronomy 32-34

NOTES AND REFLECTIONS

Study Notes

_____
_____
_____
_____
_____
_____
_____
_____
_____
_____
_____
_____

VERSE OF THE DAY DEUTERONOMY 32:4

TODAY I'M GRATEFUL FOR

1.

2.

3.

PRAYER & PRAISE

SEEKING  SCRIPTURE

NOTES AND REFLECTIONS

_____
_____
_____
_____
_____

Study Notes

_____
_____
_____
_____
_____
_____
_____

VERSE OF THE DAY JOSHUA 1:8

PRAYER & PRAISE

TODAY I'M GRATEFUL FOR

1.

2.

3.

SEEKING SCRIPTURE

DAY 71

Joshua 5-8

Study Notes

_____
_____
_____
_____
_____
_____
_____
_____
_____
_____
_____

VERSE OF THE DAY JOSHUA 6:20

PRAYER & PRAISE

TODAY I'M GRATEFUL FOR

1.

2.

3.

SEEKING  SCRIPTURE

NOTES AND REFLECTIONS

Study Notes

VERSE OF THE DAY JOSHUA 10:13

PRAYER & PRAISE

TODAY I'M GRATEFUL FOR

1.

2.

3.

SEEKING  SCRIPTURE

DAY 73

Joshua 12-15

NOTES AND REFLECTIONS

Study Notes

VERSE OF THE DAY JOSHUA 14:9

PRAYER & PRAISE

TODAY I'M GRATEFUL FOR

1.

2.

3.

SEEKING  SCRIPTURE

NOTES AND REFLECTIONS

Study Notes

VERSE OF THE DAY JOSHUA 17:13

PRAYER & PRAISE

TODAY I'M GRATEFUL FOR

1.

2.

3.

DAY 75

Joshua 19-21

Study Notes

NOTES AND REFLECTIONS

VERSE OF THE DAY JOSHUA 21:44

PRAYER & PRAISE

TODAY I'M GRATEFUL FOR

1.

2.

3.

SEEKING  SCRIPTURE

NOTES AND REFLECTIONS

_____

_____

_____

_____

_____

_____

_____

_____

_____

_____

_____

Study Notes

VERSE OF THE DAY JOSHUA 24:15

PRAYER & PRAISE

TODAY I'M GRATEFUL FOR

1.

2.

3.

SEEKING SCRIPTURE

DAY 77

Judges 1-2

Study Notes

_____
_____
_____
_____
_____
_____
_____
_____
_____
_____
_____
_____
_____

VERSE OF THE DAY JUDGES 2:10

PRAYER & PRAISE

TODAY I'M GRATEFUL FOR

1.

2.

3.

SEEKING  SCRIPTURE

NOTES AND REFLECTIONS

Judges 3-5

Study Notes

VERSE OF THE DAY JUDGES 3:7

PRAYER & PRAISE

TODAY I'M GRATEFUL FOR

1.

2.

3.

SEEKING SCRIPTURE

DAY 79

Judges 6-7

Study Notes

NOTES AND REFLECTIONS

VERSE OF THE DAY JUDGES 6:22

TODAY I'M GRATEFUL FOR

1.

2.

3.

PRAYER & PRAISE

DAY 80

Judges 8-9

NOTES AND REFLECTIONS

Study Notes

_____
_____
_____
_____
_____
_____
_____
_____
_____
_____
_____
_____

VERSE OF THE DAY JUDGES 8:23

PRAYER & PRAISE

TODAY I'M GRATEFUL FOR

1.

2.

3.

SEEKING  SCRIPTURE

DAY 81

Judges 10-12

NOTES AND REFLECTIONS

_____
_____
_____
_____

Study Notes

_____
_____
_____
_____
_____
_____
_____
_____

VERSE OF THE DAY JUDGES 10:16

_____
_____
_____
_____
_____
_____
_____

PRAYER & PRAISE

TODAY I'M GRATEFUL FOR

1.

2.

3.

SEEKING  SCRIPTURE

NOTES AND REFLECTIONS

Study Notes

VERSE OF THE DAY JUDGES 13:18

PRAYER & PRAISE

TODAY I'M GRATEFUL FOR

1.

2.

3.

SEEKING  SCRIPTURE

DAY 83

Judges 16-18

NOTES AND REFLECTIONS

Study Notes

VERSE OF THE DAY JUDGES 16:19

PRAYER & PRAISE

TODAY I'M GRATEFUL FOR

1.

2.

3.

SEEKING  SCRIPTURE

NOTES AND REFLECTIONS

Study Notes

VERSE OF THE DAY JUDGES 21:25

PRAYER & PRAISE

TODAY I'M GRATEFUL FOR

1.

2.

3.

SEEKING SCRIPTURE

DAY 85

Ruth 1-4

Study Notes

VERSE OF THE DAY RUTH 1:16

PRAYER & PRAISE

TODAY I'M GRATEFUL FOR

1.

2.

3.

SEEKING  SCRIPTURE

DAY 86

NOTES AND REFLECTIONS

1 Samuel 1-3

Study Notes

VERSE OF THE DAY 1 SAMUEL 2:2

PRAYER & PRAISE

TODAY I'M GRATEFUL FOR

1.

2.

3.

DAY 87

1 Samuel 4-8

NOTES AND REFLECTIONS

Study Notes

VERSE OF THE DAY 1 SAMUEL 8:7

PRAYER & PRAISE

TODAY I'M GRATEFUL FOR

1.

2.

3.

DAY 88

1 Samuel 9-12

NOTES AND REFLECTIONS

_____

_____

_____

_____

_____

Study Notes

_____

_____

_____

_____

_____

_____

VERSE OF THE DAY 1 SAMUEL 12:21

PRAYER & PRAISE

TODAY I'M GRATEFUL FOR

1.

2.

3.

SEEKING  SCRIPTURE

DAY 89

1 Samuel 13-14

NOTES AND REFLECTIONS

Study Notes

_____

VERSE OF THE DAY 1 SAMUEL 13:14

PRAYER & PRAISE

TODAY I'M GRATEFUL FOR

1.

2.

3.

SEEKING  SCRIPTURE

NOTES AND REFLECTIONS

Study Notes

VERSE OF THE DAY 1 SAMUEL 15:22

PRAYER & PRAISE

TODAY I'M GRATEFUL FOR

1.

2.

3.

SEEKING  SCRIPTURE

DAY 91

1 Samuel 18-20

NOTES AND REFLECTIONS

Study Notes

_____
_____
_____
_____
_____

_____
_____
_____
_____
_____
_____
_____

VERSE OF THE DAY 1 SAMUEL 18:14

PRAYER & PRAISE

TODAY I'M GRATEFUL FOR

1.

2.

3.

SEEKING  SCRIPTURE

NOTES AND REFLECTIONS

Study Notes

VERSE OF THE DAY 1 SAMUEL 24:12

PRAYER & PRAISE

TODAY I'M GRATEFUL FOR

1.

2.

3.

SEEKING  SCRIPTURE

DAY 93

1 Samuel 25-27

NOTES AND REFLECTIONS

Study Notes

_____
_____
_____
_____
_____

_____
_____
_____
_____
_____
_____

VERSE OF THE DAY 1 SAMUEL 25:33

PRAYER & PRAISE

TODAY I'M GRATEFUL FOR

1.

2.

3.

SEEKING  SCRIPTURE

NOTES AND REFLECTIONS

Study Notes

VERSE OF THE DAY 1 SAMUEL 30:23

PRAYER & PRAISE

TODAY I'M GRATEFUL FOR

1.

2.

3.

DAY 95

2 Samuel 1-3

NOTES AND REFLECTIONS

Study Notes

VERSE OF THE DAY 2 SAMUEL 2:7

PRAYER & PRAISE

TODAY I'M GRATEFUL FOR

1.

2.

3.

SEEKING  SCRIPTURE

NOTES AND REFLECTIONS

_____

_____

_____

_____

_____

_____

_____

_____

_____

_____

_____

_____

Study Notes

VERSE OF THE DAY 2 SAMUEL 5:10

PRAYER & PRAISE

TODAY I'M GRATEFUL FOR

1.

2.

3.

SEEKING  SCRIPTURE

DAY 97

2 Samuel 8-12

NOTES AND REFLECTIONS

Study Notes

_____

VERSE OF THE DAY 2 SAMUEL 12:5

PRAYER & PRAISE

TODAY I'M GRATEFUL FOR

1.

2.

3.

SEEKING  SCRIPTURE

NOTES AND REFLECTIONS

Study Notes

VERSE OF THE DAY 2 SAMUEL 15:25

PRAYER & PRAISE

TODAY I'M GRATEFUL FOR

1.

2.

3.

SEEKING  SCRIPTURE

DAY 99

2 Samuel 16-18

NOTES AND REFLECTIONS

Study Notes

_____

_____

_____

_____

_____

_____

_____

_____

_____

_____

_____

_____

VERSE OF THE DAY 2 SAMUEL 18:9

TODAY I'M GRATEFUL FOR

1.

2.

3.

PRAYER & PRAISE

SEEKING SCRIPTURE

DAY 100
2 Samuel 19-21

NOTES AND REFLECTIONS

_____
_____
_____
_____
_____

Study Notes

_____
_____
_____
_____
_____
_____

VERSE OF THE DAY 2 SAMUEL 19:7

PRAYER & PRAISE

TODAY I'M GRATEFUL FOR

1.

2.

3.

DAY 101

2 Samuel 22-24

NOTES AND REFLECTIONS

Study Notes

_____

_____

_____

_____

_____

_____

_____

_____

_____

_____

_____

VERSE OF THE DAY 2 SAMUEL 22:31- 32

PRAYER & PRAISE

TODAY I'M GRATEFUL FOR

1.

2.

3.

SEEKING SCRIPTURE

NOTES AND REFLECTIONS

Study Notes

VERSE OF THE DAY 1 KINGS 2:2

PRAYER & PRAISE

TODAY I'M GRATEFUL FOR

1.

2.

3.

SEEKING SCRIPTURE

DAY 103

1 Kings 3-5

Study Notes

VERSE OF THE DAY 1 KINGS 3:9

PRAYER & PRAISE

TODAY I'M GRATEFUL FOR

1.

2.

3.

SEEKING 💡 SCRIPTURE

NOTES AND REFLECTIONS

Study Notes

_____

_____

_____

_____

_____

_____

_____

_____

_____

_____

_____

_____

VERSE OF THE DAY 1 KINGS 6:12-13

PRAYER & PRAISE

TODAY I'M GRATEFUL FOR

1.

2.

3.

SEEKING SCRIPTURE

DAY 105

1 Kings 8-9

Study Notes

_____
_____
_____
_____
_____

_____
_____
_____
_____
_____
_____

VERSE OF THE DAY 1 KINGS 8:61

PRAYER & PRAISE

TODAY I'M GRATEFUL FOR

1.

2.

3.

SEEKING  SCRIPTURE

NOTES AND REFLECTIONS

_____
_____
_____
_____
_____

Study Notes

_____
_____
_____
_____
_____
_____
_____

VERSE OF THE DAY 1 KINGS 11:4

PRAYER & PRAISE

TODAY I'M GRATEFUL FOR

1.

2.

3.

SEEKING  SCRIPTURE

DAY 107

1 Kings 12-14

NOTES AND REFLECTIONS

Study Notes

_____

_____

_____

_____

_____

_____

_____

_____

_____

_____

_____

VERSE OF THE DAY 1 KINGS 14:15

TODAY I'M GRATEFUL FOR

1.

2.

3.

PRAYER & PRAISE

SEEKING  SCRIPTURE

NOTES AND REFLECTIONS

Study Notes

VERSE OF THE DAY 1 KINGS 17:1

PRAYER & PRAISE

TODAY I'M GRATEFUL FOR

1.

2.

3.

DAY 109

1 Kings 18-20

NOTES AND REFLECTIONS

Study Notes

_____
_____
_____
_____
_____
_____
_____
_____
_____
_____
_____
_____

VERSE OF THE DAY 1 KINGS 19:12

TODAY I'M GRATEFUL FOR

1.

2.

3.

PRAYER & PRAISE

SEEKING  SCRIPTURE

NOTES AND REFLECTIONS

_____
_____
_____
_____
_____

Study Notes

_____
_____
_____
_____
_____
_____
_____

VERSE OF THE DAY 1 KINGS 22:17

PRAYER & PRAISE

TODAY I'M GRATEFUL FOR

1.

2.

3.

SEEKING  SCRIPTURE

DAY 111

2 Kings 1-3

Study Notes

NOTES AND REFLECTIONS

_____
_____
_____
_____
_____
_____
_____
_____
_____
_____
_____
_____

VERSE OF THE DAY 2 KINGS 2:10

TODAY I'M GRATEFUL FOR

1.

2.

3.

PRAYER & PRAISE

SEEKING  SCRIPTURE

NOTES AND REFLECTIONS

Study Notes

VERSE OF THE DAY 2 KINGS 4:6

PRAYER & PRAISE

TODAY I'M GRATEFUL FOR

1.

2.

3.

SEEKING  SCRIPTURE

DAY 113

2 Kings 6-8

NOTES AND REFLECTIONS

Study Notes

_____
_____
_____
_____
_____
_____
_____
_____
_____
_____
_____
_____

VERSE OF THE DAY 2 KINGS 6:16

PRAYER & PRAISE

TODAY I'M GRATEFUL FOR

1.

2.

3.

NOTES AND REFLECTIONS

_____
_____
_____
_____
_____

Study Notes

_____
_____
_____
_____
_____
_____
_____

VERSE OF THE DAY 2 KINGS 10:31

PRAYER & PRAISE

TODAY I'M GRATEFUL FOR

1.

2.

3.

SEEKING  SCRIPTURE

DAY 115

2 Kings 12-14

Study Notes

_____
_____
_____
_____
_____
_____
_____
_____
_____
_____
_____
_____

VERSE OF THE DAY 2 KINGS 13:21

PRAYER & PRAISE

TODAY I'M GRATEFUL FOR

1.

2.

3.

SEEKING  SCRIPTURE

NOTES AND REFLECTIONS

_____

_____

_____

_____

_____

_____

_____

_____

_____

_____

_____

Study Notes

VERSE OF THE DAY 2 KINGS 17:13

PRAYER & PRAISE

TODAY I'M GRATEFUL FOR

1.

2.

3.

SEEKING  SCRIPTURE

DAY 117

2 Kings 18-19

NOTES AND REFLECTIONS

Study Notes

_____

_____

_____

_____

_____

_____

_____

_____

_____

_____

_____

VERSE OF THE DAY 2 KINGS 18:6-7

PRAYER & PRAISE

TODAY I'M GRATEFUL FOR

1.

2.

3.

SEEKING  SCRIPTURE

NOTES AND REFLECTIONS

_____
_____
_____
_____
_____

Study Notes

_____
_____
_____
_____
_____
_____

VERSE OF THE DAY 2 KINGS 20:9-10

PRAYER & PRAISE

TODAY I'M GRATEFUL FOR

1.

2.

3.

SEEKING  SCRIPTURE

DAY 119

2 Kings 23-25

NOTES AND REFLECTIONS

Study Notes

_____

VERSE OF THE DAY 2 KINGS 23:3

PRAYER & PRAISE

TODAY I'M GRATEFUL FOR

1.

2.

3.

SEEKING  SCRIPTURE

NOTES AND REFLECTIONS

Study Notes

VERSE OF THE DAY 1 CHRONICLES 2:1-2

PRAYER & PRAISE

TODAY I'M GRATEFUL FOR

1.

2.

3.

SEEKING SCRIPTURE

DAY 121

1 Chronicles 3-5

NOTES AND REFLECTIONS

Study Notes

_____
_____
_____
_____
_____
_____
_____
_____
_____
_____
_____
_____

VERSE OF THE DAY 1 CHRONICLES 4:10

PRAYER & PRAISE

TODAY I'M GRATEFUL FOR

1.

2.

3.

SEEKING  SCRIPTURE

NOTES AND REFLECTIONS

_____
_____
_____
_____
_____

Study Notes

_____
_____
_____
_____
_____
_____
_____

VERSE OF THE DAY 1 CHRONICLES 6:49

PRAYER & PRAISE

TODAY I'M GRATEFUL FOR

1.

2.

3.

SEEKING  SCRIPTURE

DAY 123

1 Chronicles 7-8

NOTES AND REFLECTIONS

_____

_____

_____

_____

_____

Study Notes

_____

_____

_____

_____

_____

_____

VERSE OF THE DAY 1 CHRONICLES 8:33

PRAYER & PRAISE

TODAY I'M GRATEFUL FOR

1.

2.

3.

SEEKING  SCRIPTURE

NOTES AND REFLECTIONS

Study Notes

VERSE OF THE DAY 1 CHRONICLES 11:14

PRAYER & PRAISE

TODAY I'M GRATEFUL FOR

1.

2.

3.

SEEKING  SCRIPTURE

DAY 125

1 Chronicles 12-14

NOTES AND REFLECTIONS

Study Notes

VERSE OF THE DAY 1 CHRONICLES 12:18

PRAYER & PRAISE

TODAY I'M GRATEFUL FOR

1.

2.

3.

SEEKING  SCRIPTURE

NOTES AND REFLECTIONS

Study Notes

VERSE OF THE DAY 1 CHRONICLES 16:9

PRAYER & PRAISE

TODAY I'M GRATEFUL FOR

1.

2.

3.

SEEKING  SCRIPTURE

DAY 127

1 Chronicles 18-21

NOTES AND REFLECTIONS

Study Notes

_____

_____

_____

_____

_____

_____

_____

_____

_____

_____

_____

_____

VERSE OF THE DAY 1 CHRONICLES 21:8

PRAYER & PRAISE

TODAY I'M GRATEFUL FOR

1.

2.

3.

SEEKING  SCRIPTURE

NOTES AND REFLECTIONS

Study Notes

VERSE OF THE DAY 1 CHRONICLES 22:12-13

PRAYER & PRAISE

TODAY I'M GRATEFUL FOR

1.

2.

3.

SEEKING  SCRIPTURE

DAY 129

1 Chronicles 25-27

NOTES AND REFLECTIONS

Study Notes

VERSE OF THE DAY 1 CHRONICLES 27:23

PRAYER & PRAISE

TODAY I'M GRATEFUL FOR

1.

2.

3.

SEEKING  SCRIPTURE

NOTES AND REFLECTIONS

Study Notes

VERSE OF THE DAY 1 CHRONICLES 28:9

PRAYER & PRAISE

TODAY I'M GRATEFUL FOR

1.

2.

3.

DAY 131

2 Chronicles 2-5

NOTES AND REFLECTIONS

Study Notes

VERSE OF THE DAY 2 CHRONICLES 5:13

PRAYER & PRAISE

TODAY I'M GRATEFUL FOR

1.

2.

3.

SEEKING  SCRIPTURE

NOTES AND REFLECTIONS

Study Notes

VERSE OF THE DAY 2 CHRONICLES 7:14

PRAYER & PRAISE

TODAY I'M GRATEFUL FOR

1.

2.

3.

SEEKING  SCRIPTURE

DAY 133

2 Chronicles 9-12

Study Notes

NOTES AND REFLECTIONS

_____
_____
_____
_____
_____

_____
_____
_____
_____
_____
_____
_____

VERSE OF THE DAY 2 CHRONICLES 10:8

PRAYER & PRAISE

TODAY I'M GRATEFUL FOR

1.

2.

3.

SEEKING  SCRIPTURE

NOTES AND REFLECTIONS

Study Notes

VERSE OF THE DAY 2 CHRONICLES 14:11

PRAYER & PRAISE

TODAY I'M GRATEFUL FOR

1.

2.

3.

SEEKING  SCRIPTURE

DAY 135

2 Chronicles 18-20

NOTES AND REFLECTIONS

Study Notes

VERSE OF THE DAY 2 CHRONICLES 20:15

PRAYER & PRAISE

TODAY I'M GRATEFUL FOR

1.

2.

3.

SEEKING  SCRIPTURE

NOTES AND REFLECTIONS

_____
_____
_____
_____
_____

Study Notes

_____
_____
_____
_____
_____
_____
_____

VERSE OF THE DAY 2 CHRONICLES 24:8

PRAYER & PRAISE

TODAY I'M GRATEFUL FOR

1.

2.

3.

SEEKING  SCRIPTURE

DAY 137

2 Chronicles 25-27

NOTES AND REFLECTIONS

Study Notes

VERSE OF THE DAY 2 CHRONICLES 25:2

PRAYER & PRAISE

TODAY I'M GRATEFUL FOR

1.

2.

3.

SEEKING  SCRIPTURE

NOTES AND REFLECTIONS

Study Notes

VERSE OF THE DAY 2 CHRONICLES 31:1

PRAYER & PRAISE

TODAY I'M GRATEFUL FOR

1.

2.

3.

SEEKING  SCRIPTURE

DAY 139

2 Chronicles 32-34

NOTES AND REFLECTIONS

Study Notes

_____
_____
_____
_____
_____
_____
_____
_____
_____
_____
_____
_____

VERSE OF THE DAY 2 CHRONICLES 34:31

PRAYER & PRAISE

TODAY I'M GRATEFUL FOR

1.

2.

3.

SEEKING  SCRIPTURE

NOTES AND REFLECTIONS

Study Notes

VERSE OF THE DAY 2 CHRONICLES 35:16

PRAYER & PRAISE

TODAY I'M GRATEFUL FOR

1.

2.

3.

SEEKING  SCRIPTURE

DAY 141

Ezra 1-3

Study Notes

NOTES AND REFLECTIONS

_____

_____

_____

_____

_____

_____

_____

_____

_____

_____

_____

_____

VERSE OF THE DAY EZRA 3:6

TODAY I'M GRATEFUL FOR

1.

2.

3.

PRAYER & PRAISE

SEEKING SCRIPTURE

Ezra 4-7

NOTES AND REFLECTIONS

_____
_____
_____
_____
_____

Study Notes

_____
_____
_____
_____
_____
_____

VERSE OF THE DAY EZRA 7:10

PRAYER & PRAISE

TODAY I'M GRATEFUL FOR

1.

2.

3.

DAY 143

Ezra 8-10

Study Notes

NOTES AND REFLECTIONS

_____
_____
_____
_____
_____
_____
_____
_____
_____
_____
_____

VERSE OF THE DAY EZRA 9:15

PRAYER & PRAISE

TODAY I'M GRATEFUL FOR

1.

2.

3.

SEEKING  SCRIPTURE

NOTES AND REFLECTIONS

Study Notes

VERSE OF THE DAY NEHEMIAH 1:7

PRAYER & PRAISE

TODAY I'M GRATEFUL FOR

1.

2.

3.

SEEKING  SCRIPTURE

DAY 145

Nehemiah 4-6

NOTES AND REFLECTIONS

Study Notes

_____
_____
_____
_____
_____

_____
_____
_____
_____
_____
_____

VERSE OF THE DAY NEHEMIAH 4:14

PRAYER & PRAISE

TODAY I'M GRATEFUL FOR

1.

2.

3.

DAY 146

NOTES AND REFLECTIONS

Nehemiah 7

Study Notes

_____
_____
_____
_____
_____
_____
_____
_____
_____
_____
_____

VERSE OF THE DAY NEHEMIAH 7:2

PRAYER & PRAISE

TODAY I'M GRATEFUL FOR

1.

2.

3.

SEEKING  SCRIPTURE

DAY 147
Nehemiah 8-9

NOTES AND REFLECTIONS

Study Notes

VERSE OF THE DAY NEHEMIAH 8:10

PRAYER & PRAISE

TODAY I'M GRATEFUL FOR

1.

2.

3.

SEEKING  SCRIPTURE

NOTES AND REFLECTIONS

Study Notes

VERSE OF THE DAY NEHEMIAH 11:2

PRAYER & PRAISE

TODAY I'M GRATEFUL FOR

1.

2.

3.

SEEKING  SCRIPTURE

DAY 149

Nehemiah 12-13

Study Notes

NOTES AND REFLECTIONS

_____
_____
_____
_____
_____
_____
_____
_____
_____
_____
_____

VERSE OF THE DAY NEHEMIAH 12:43

PRAYER & PRAISE

TODAY I'M GRATEFUL FOR

1.

2.

3.

SEEKING  SCRIPTURE

NOTES AND REFLECTIONS

Study Notes

VERSE OF THE DAY ESTHER 4:14

PRAYER & PRAISE

TODAY I'M GRATEFUL FOR

1.

2.

3.

SEEKING  SCRIPTURE

DAY 151

Esther 6-10

Study Notes

NOTES AND REFLECTIONS

_____
_____
_____
_____
_____
_____
_____
_____
_____
_____
_____
_____
_____

VERSE OF THE DAY ESTHER 9:2

TODAY I'M GRATEFUL FOR

1.

2.

3.

PRAYER & PRAISE

SEEKING  SCRIPTURE

NOTES AND REFLECTIONS

Study Notes

VERSE OF THE DAY JOB 1:20-21

PRAYER & PRAISE

TODAY I'M GRATEFUL FOR

1.

2.

3.

SEEKING  SCRIPTURE

DAY 153

Job 5-7

Study Notes

NOTES AND REFLECTIONS

_____
_____
_____
_____
_____

_____
_____
_____
_____
_____
_____

VERSE OF THE DAY JOB 5:17

PRAYER & PRAISE

TODAY I'M GRATEFUL FOR

1.

2.

3.

SEEKING SCRIPTURE

NOTES AND REFLECTIONS

Study Notes

VERSE OF THE DAY JOB 9:8-9

PRAYER & PRAISE

TODAY I'M GRATEFUL FOR

1.

2.

3.

SEEKING  SCRIPTURE

DAY 155

Job 11-13

NOTES AND REFLECTIONS

Study Notes

VERSE OF THE DAY JOB 13:15

PRAYER & PRAISE

TODAY I'M GRATEFUL FOR

1.

2.

3.

SEEKING  SCRIPTURE

DAY 156
Job 14-16

NOTES AND REFLECTIONS

Study Notes

VERSE OF THE DAY JOB 15:31

PRAYER & PRAISE

TODAY I'M GRATEFUL FOR

1.

2.

3.

DAY 157

Job 17-20

NOTES AND REFLECTIONS

Study Notes

_____

_____

_____

_____

_____

_____

_____

_____

_____

_____

_____

_____

VERSE OF THE DAY JOB 19:25

PRAYER & PRAISE

TODAY I'M GRATEFUL FOR

1.

2.

3.

SEEKING SCRIPTURE

NOTES AND REFLECTIONS

Study Notes

VERSE OF THE DAY JOB 23:12

PRAYER & PRAISE

TODAY I'M GRATEFUL FOR

1.

2.

3.

SEEKING SCRIPTURE

DAY 159

Job 24-28

Study Notes

_____
_____
_____
_____
_____
_____
_____
_____
_____
_____
_____
_____
_____
_____

VERSE OF THE DAY JOB 28:28

PRAYER & PRAISE

TODAY I'M GRATEFUL FOR

1.

2.

3.

SEEKING SCRIPTURE

NOTES AND REFLECTIONS

Study Notes

VERSE OF THE DAY JOB 29:4

PRAYER & PRAISE

TODAY I'M GRATEFUL FOR

1.

2.

3.

SEEKING  SCRIPTURE

DAY 161

Job 32-34

Study Notes

NOTES AND REFLECTIONS

_____
_____
_____
_____
_____
_____
_____
_____
_____
_____
_____
_____
_____

VERSE OF THE DAY JOB 34:3-4

PRAYER & PRAISE

TODAY I'M GRATEFUL FOR

1.

2.

3.

SEEKING SCRIPTURE

NOTES AND REFLECTIONS

Study Notes

VERSE OF THE DAY JOB 36:10

PRAYER & PRAISE

TODAY I'M GRATEFUL FOR

1.

2.

3.

SEEKING  SCRIPTURE

DAY 163

Job 38-39

Study Notes

NOTES AND REFLECTIONS

_____

_____

_____

_____

_____

_____

_____

_____

_____

_____

_____

VERSE OF THE DAY JOB 40:6-7

PRAYER & PRAISE

TODAY I'M GRATEFUL FOR

1.

2.

3.

SEEKING SCRIPTURE

NOTES AND REFLECTIONS

Job 40-42

Study Notes

_____
_____
_____
_____
_____
_____
_____
_____
_____
_____
_____

VERSE OF THE DAY JOB 42:10

PRAYER & PRAISE

TODAY I'M GRATEFUL FOR

1.

2.

3.

SEEKING SCRIPTURE

DAY 165

Psalm 1-8

NOTES AND REFLECTIONS

_____

_____

_____

_____

Study Notes

_____

_____

_____

_____

_____

_____

_____

VERSE OF THE DAY PSALM 1:1

PRAYER & PRAISE

TODAY I'M GRATEFUL FOR

1.

2.

3.

SEEKING SCRIPTURE

NOTES AND REFLECTIONS

Study Notes

VERSE OF THE DAY PSALM 9:1

PRAYER & PRAISE

TODAY I'M GRATEFUL FOR

1.

2.

3.

SEEKING  SCRIPTURE

DAY 167

Psalm 17-20

NOTES AND REFLECTIONS

Study Notes

_____
_____
_____
_____
_____
_____
_____
_____
_____
_____
_____
_____

VERSE OF THE DAY PSALM 19:7

PRAYER & PRAISE

TODAY I'M GRATEFUL FOR

1.

2.

3.

SEEKING  SCRIPTURE

NOTES AND REFLECTIONS

Study Notes

_____

VERSE OF THE DAY PSALM 25:4-5

PRAYER & PRAISE

TODAY I'M GRATEFUL FOR

1.

2.

3.

SEEKING  SCRIPTURE

DAY 169

Psalm 26-31

Study Notes

NOTES AND REFLECTIONS

_____
_____
_____
_____
_____
_____
_____
_____
_____
_____
_____

VERSE OF THE DAY PSALM 26:1-2

TODAY I'M GRATEFUL FOR

1.

2.

3.

PRAYER & PRAISE

SEEKING  SCRIPTURE

NOTES AND REFLECTIONS

Study Notes

VERSE OF THE DAY PSALM 33:18

PRAYER & PRAISE

TODAY I'M GRATEFUL FOR

1.

2.

3.

SEEKING SCRIPTURE

DAY 171

Psalm 36-39

Study Notes

VERSE OF THE DAY PSALM 36:7

PRAYER & PRAISE

TODAY I'M GRATEFUL FOR

1.

2.

3.

SEEKING  SCRIPTURE

NOTES AND REFLECTIONS

Study Notes

VERSE OF THE DAY PSALM 40:16

PRAYER & PRAISE

TODAY I'M GRATEFUL FOR

1.

2.

3.

SEEKING SCRIPTURE

DAY 173

Psalm 46-50

Study Notes

VERSE OF THE DAY PSALM 48:10

PRAYER & PRAISE

TODAY I'M GRATEFUL FOR

1.

2.

3.

SEEKING SCRIPTURE

NOTES AND REFLECTIONS

Study Notes

VERSE OF THE DAY PSALM 56:4

PRAYER & PRAISE

TODAY I'M GRATEFUL FOR

1.

2.

3.

SEEKING  SCRIPTURE

DAY 175

Psalm 58-65

Study Notes

VERSE OF THE DAY PSALM 62:11-12

PRAYER & PRAISE

TODAY I'M GRATEFUL FOR

1.

2.

3.

SEEKING  SCRIPTURE

NOTES AND REFLECTIONS

_____
_____
_____
_____
_____

Study Notes

_____
_____
_____
_____
_____
_____

VERSE OF THE DAY PSALM 66:16

PRAYER & PRAISE

TODAY I'M GRATEFUL FOR

1.

2.

3.

DAY 177

Psalm 70-73

NOTES AND REFLECTIONS

Study Notes

_____

_____

_____

_____

_____

_____

_____

_____

_____

_____

_____

_____

VERSE OF THE DAY PSALM 71:19

TODAY I'M GRATEFUL FOR

1.

2.

3.

PRAYER & PRAISE

SEEKING  SCRIPTURE

NOTES AND REFLECTIONS

Study Notes

VERSE OF THE DAY PSALM 77:12

PRAYER & PRAISE

TODAY I'M GRATEFUL FOR

1.

2.

3.

SEEKING  SCRIPTURE

DAY 179

Psalm 78-79

Study Notes

_____
_____
_____
_____
_____
_____
_____
_____
_____
_____
_____
_____

VERSE OF THE DAY PSALM 79:9

PRAYER & PRAISE

TODAY I'M GRATEFUL FOR

1.

2.

3.

SEEKING SCRIPTURE

NOTES AND REFLECTIONS

Study Notes

VERSE OF THE DAY PSALM 81:3

PRAYER & PRAISE

TODAY I'M GRATEFUL FOR

1.

2.

3.

SEEKING  SCRIPTURE

DAY 181

Psalm 86-89

NOTES AND REFLECTIONS

_____

VERSE OF THE DAY PSALM 86:11

PRAYER & PRAISE

TODAY I'M GRATEFUL FOR

1.

2.

3.

SEEKING  SCRIPTURE

NOTES AND REFLECTIONS

Study Notes

_____

VERSE OF THE DAY PSALM 91:4

PRAYER & PRAISE

TODAY I'M GRATEFUL FOR

1.

2.

3.

DAY 183

Psalm 96-102

NOTES AND REFLECTIONS

Study Notes

_____

_____

_____

_____

_____

_____

_____

_____

_____

_____

_____

_____

_____

VERSE OF THE DAY PSALM 98:3

PRAYER & PRAISE

TODAY I'M GRATEFUL FOR

1.

2.

3.

DAY 184

NOTES AND REFLECTIONS

Psalm 103-105

Study Notes

_____
_____
_____
_____
_____
_____
_____
_____
_____
_____
_____
_____

VERSE OF THE DAY PSALM 104:33

PRAYER & PRAISE

TODAY I'M GRATEFUL FOR

1.

2.

3.

SEEKING  SCRIPTURE

DAY 185
Psalm 106-107

NOTES AND REFLECTIONS

Study Notes

_____
_____
_____
_____
_____
_____
_____
_____
_____
_____
_____

VERSE OF THE DAY PSALM 107:9

TODAY I'M GRATEFUL FOR

1.

2.

3.

PRAYER & PRAISE

SEEKING  SCRIPTURE

NOTES AND REFLECTIONS

Study Notes

_____
_____
_____
_____
_____
_____
_____
_____
_____
_____
_____

VERSE OF THE DAY PSALM 112:1

PRAYER & PRAISE

TODAY I'M GRATEFUL FOR

1.

2.

3.

SEEKING  SCRIPTURE

DAY 187

Psalm 115-118

NOTES AND REFLECTIONS

Study Notes

_____

VERSE OF THE DAY PSALM 118:6

PRAYER & PRAISE

TODAY I'M GRATEFUL FOR

1.

2.

3.

SEEKING SCRIPTURE

NOTES AND REFLECTIONS

Study Notes

VERSE OF THE DAY PSALM 119:11

PRAYER & PRAISE

TODAY I'M GRATEFUL FOR

1.

2.

3.

SEEKING  SCRIPTURE

DAY 189

Psalm 119:89-176

Study Notes

NOTES AND REFLECTIONS

_____
_____
_____
_____
_____
_____
_____
_____
_____
_____
_____

VERSE OF THE DAY PSALM 119:97

PRAYER & PRAISE

TODAY I'M GRATEFUL FOR

1.

2.

3.

SEEKING  SCRIPTURE

NOTES AND REFLECTIONS

Psalm 120-132

Study Notes

VERSE OF THE DAY PSALM 125:2

PRAYER & PRAISE

TODAY I'M GRATEFUL FOR

1.

2.

3.

SEEKING  SCRIPTURE

DAY 191

Psalm 133-139

NOTES AND REFLECTIONS

Study Notes

VERSE OF THE DAY PSALM 133:1

PRAYER & PRAISE

TODAY I'M GRATEFUL FOR

1.

2.

3.

SEEKING SCRIPTURE

NOTES AND REFLECTIONS

Study Notes

VERSE OF THE DAY PSALM 143:10

PRAYER & PRAISE

TODAY I'M GRATEFUL FOR

1.

2.

3.

SEEKING SCRIPTURE

DAY 193

Psalm 146-150

Study Notes

VERSE OF THE DAY PSALM 149:1-2

PRAYER & PRAISE

TODAY I'M GRATEFUL FOR

1.

2.

3.

SEEKING  SCRIPTURE

NOTES AND REFLECTIONS

Proverbs 1-3

Study Notes

VERSE OF THE DAY PROVERBS 1:7

PRAYER & PRAISE

TODAY I'M GRATEFUL FOR

1.

2.

3.

SEEKING  SCRIPTURE

DAY 195

Proverbs 4-6

NOTES AND REFLECTIONS

Study Notes

VERSE OF THE DAY PROVERBS 6:16-19

PRAYER & PRAISE

TODAY I'M GRATEFUL FOR

1.

2.

3.

SEEKING  SCRIPTURE

NOTES AND REFLECTIONS

_____
_____
_____
_____
_____

Study Notes

_____
_____
_____
_____
_____
_____
_____

VERSE OF THE DAY PROVERBS 8:8

PRAYER & PRAISE

TODAY I'M GRATEFUL FOR

1.

2.

3.

SEEKING  SCRIPTURE

DAY 197

Proverbs 10-12

NOTES AND REFLECTIONS

Study Notes

VERSE OF THE DAY PROVERBS 10:2

PRAYER & PRAISE

TODAY I'M GRATEFUL FOR

1.

2.

3.

SEEKING  SCRIPTURE

Proverbs 13-15

NOTES AND REFLECTIONS

_____
_____
_____
_____
_____
_____
_____
_____
_____
_____
_____
_____

Study Notes

VERSE OF THE DAY PROVERBS 13:2-3

PRAYER & PRAISE

TODAY I'M GRATEFUL FOR

1.

2.

3.

SEEKING  SCRIPTURE

DAY 199

Proverbs 16-18

NOTES AND REFLECTIONS

Study Notes

VERSE OF THE DAY PROVERBS 16:24

TODAY I'M GRATEFUL FOR

1.

2.

3.

PRAYER & PRAISE

SEEKING  SCRIPTURE

NOTES AND REFLECTIONS

Proverbs 19-21

Study Notes

VERSE OF THE DAY PROVERBS 19:11

PRAYER & PRAISE

TODAY I'M GRATEFUL FOR

1.

2.

3.

SEEKING  SCRIPTURE

DAY 201

Proverbs 22-23

NOTES AND REFLECTIONS

Study Notes

VERSE OF THE DAY PROVERBS 22:8

PRAYER & PRAISE

TODAY I'M GRATEFUL FOR

1.

2.

3.

SEEKING  SCRIPTURE

NOTES AND REFLECTIONS

Proverbs 24-26

Study Notes

VERSE OF THE DAY PROVERBS 24:17

PRAYER & PRAISE

TODAY I'M GRATEFUL FOR

1.

2.

3.

SEEKING  SCRIPTURE

DAY 203

Proverbs 27-29

Study Notes

NOTES AND REFLECTIONS

VERSE OF THE DAY PROVERBS 27:2

PRAYER & PRAISE

TODAY I'M GRATEFUL FOR

1.

2.

3.

SEEKING  SCRIPTURE

NOTES AND REFLECTIONS

Proverbs 30-31

Study Notes

VERSE OF THE DAY PROVERBS 30:8

PRAYER & PRAISE

TODAY I'M GRATEFUL FOR

1.

2.

3.

SEEKING  SCRIPTURE

DAY 205

Ecclesiastes 1-4

NOTES AND REFLECTIONS

Study Notes

_____
_____
_____
_____
_____

_____
_____
_____
_____
_____
_____

VERSE OF THE DAY ECCLESIASTES 2:13

PRAYER & PRAISE

TODAY I'M GRATEFUL FOR

1.

2.

3.

SEEKING  SCRIPTURE

NOTES AND REFLECTIONS

Study Notes

VERSE OF THE DAY ECCLESIASTES 7:21-22

PRAYER & PRAISE

TODAY I'M GRATEFUL FOR

1.

2.

3.

SEEKING SCRIPTURE

DAY 207

Ecclesiastes 9-12

NOTES AND REFLECTIONS

Study Notes

_____

VERSE OF THE DAY ECCLESIASTES 9:17-18

PRAYER & PRAISE

TODAY I'M GRATEFUL FOR

1.

2.

3.

SEEKING  SCRIPTURE

NOTES AND REFLECTIONS

Solomon 1-8

Study Notes

VERSE OF THE DAY SOLOMON 8:6

PRAYER & PRAISE

TODAY I'M GRATEFUL FOR

1.

2.

3.

SEEKING  SCRIPTURE

DAY 209

Isaiah 1-4

Study Notes

VERSE OF THE DAY ISAIAH 2:3

PRAYER & PRAISE

TODAY I'M GRATEFUL FOR

1.

2.

3.

SEEKING  SCRIPTURE

Isaiah 5-8

NOTES AND REFLECTIONS

_____
_____
_____
_____
_____

Study Notes

_____
_____
_____
_____
_____
_____
_____

VERSE OF THE DAY ISAIAH 5:13

PRAYER & PRAISE

TODAY I'M GRATEFUL FOR

1.

2.

3.

SEEKING SCRIPTURE

DAY 211

Isaiah 9-12

Study Notes

NOTES AND REFLECTIONS

_____
_____
_____
_____
_____
_____
_____
_____
_____
_____
_____

VERSE OF THE DAY ISAIAH 12:2

TODAY I'M GRATEFUL FOR

1.

2.

3.

PRAYER & PRAISE

SEEKING  SCRIPTURE

NOTES AND REFLECTIONS

Study Notes

VERSE OF THE DAY ISAIAH 17:7

PRAYER & PRAISE

TODAY I'M GRATEFUL FOR

1.

2.

3.

SEEKING  SCRIPTURE

DAY 213

Isaiah 18-22

NOTES AND REFLECTIONS

Study Notes

VERSE OF THE DAY ISAIAH 18:3

PRAYER & PRAISE

TODAY I'M GRATEFUL FOR

1.

2.

3.

DAY 214

NOTES AND REFLECTIONS

Isaiah 23-27

Study Notes

_____
_____
_____
_____
_____
_____
_____
_____
_____
_____
_____
_____

VERSE OF THE DAY ISAIAH 26:3

PRAYER & PRAISE

TODAY I'M GRATEFUL FOR

1.

2.

3.

DAY 215

Isaiah 28-30

NOTES AND REFLECTIONS

Study Notes

_____
_____
_____
_____
_____
_____

_____
_____
_____
_____
_____
_____

VERSE OF THE DAY ISAIAH 29:16

PRAYER & PRAISE

TODAY I'M GRATEFUL FOR

1.

2.

3.

SEEKING SCRIPTURE

NOTES AND REFLECTIONS

Study Notes

_____

_____

_____

_____

_____

_____

_____

_____

_____

_____

_____

VERSE OF THE DAY ISAIAH 32:17-18

PRAYER & PRAISE

TODAY I'M GRATEFUL FOR

1.

2.

3.

SEEKING SCRIPTURE

DAY 217

Isaiah 36-41

Study Notes

VERSE OF THE DAY ISAIAH 41:10

PRAYER & PRAISE

TODAY I'M GRATEFUL FOR

1.

2.

3.

SEEKING  SCRIPTURE

NOTES AND REFLECTIONS

Study Notes

_____

VERSE OF THE DAY ISAIAH 43:3

PRAYER & PRAISE

TODAY I'M GRATEFUL FOR

1.

2.

3.

SEEKING  SCRIPTURE

DAY 219

Isaiah 45-48

NOTES AND REFLECTIONS

Study Notes

_____

VERSE OF THE DAY ISAIAH 48:17

PRAYER & PRAISE

TODAY I'M GRATEFUL FOR

1.

2.

3.

SEEKING  SCRIPTURE

NOTES AND REFLECTIONS

Isaiah 49-53

Study Notes

VERSE OF THE DAY ISAIAH 50:4

PRAYER & PRAISE

TODAY I'M GRATEFUL FOR

1.

2.

3.

SEEKING  SCRIPTURE

DAY 221

Isaiah 54-58

NOTES AND REFLECTIONS

Study Notes

_____
_____
_____
_____
_____
_____
_____
_____
_____
_____
_____
_____

VERSE OF THE DAY ISAIAH 56:7

PRAYER & PRAISE

TODAY I'M GRATEFUL FOR

1.

2.

3.

SEEKING  SCRIPTURE

NOTES AND REFLECTIONS

Study Notes

VERSE OF THE DAY ISAIAH 63:15

PRAYER & PRAISE

TODAY I'M GRATEFUL FOR

1.

2.

3.

DAY 223

Isaiah 64-66

NOTES AND REFLECTIONS

Study Notes

_____
_____
_____
_____
_____
_____
_____
_____
_____
_____
_____
_____

VERSE OF THE DAY ISAIAH 65:2

PRAYER & PRAISE

TODAY I'M GRATEFUL FOR

1.

2.

3.

SEEKING  SCRIPTURE

NOTES AND REFLECTIONS

Study Notes

VERSE OF THE DAY JEREMIAH 2:17

PRAYER & PRAISE

TODAY I'M GRATEFUL FOR

1.

2.

3.

SEEKING  SCRIPTURE

DAY 225

Jeremiah 4-6

NOTES AND REFLECTIONS

Study Notes

_____

VERSE OF THE DAY JEREMIAH 6:16

PRAYER & PRAISE

TODAY I'M GRATEFUL FOR

1.

2.

3.

SEEKING  SCRIPTURE

Jeremiah 7-9

NOTES AND REFLECTIONS

Study Notes

VERSE OF THE DAY JEREMIAH 7:23

PRAYER & PRAISE

TODAY I'M GRATEFUL FOR

1.

2.

3.

SEEKING  SCRIPTURE

DAY 227
Jeremiah 10-13

NOTES AND REFLECTIONS

Study Notes

VERSE OF THE DAY JEREMIAH 11:14

PRAYER & PRAISE

TODAY I'M GRATEFUL FOR

1.

2.

3.

NOTES AND REFLECTIONS

Study Notes

VERSE OF THE DAY JEREMIAH 17:9-10

PRAYER & PRAISE

TODAY I'M GRATEFUL FOR

1.

2.

3.

SEEKING  SCRIPTURE

DAY 229

Jeremiah 18-22

NOTES AND REFLECTIONS

Study Notes

_____

VERSE OF THE DAY JEREMIAH 21:8

TODAY I'M GRATEFUL FOR

1.

2.

3.

PRAYER & PRAISE

SEEKING  SCRIPTURE

NOTES AND REFLECTIONS

Study Notes

VERSE OF THE DAY JEREMIAH 23:16

PRAYER & PRAISE

TODAY I'M GRATEFUL FOR

1.

2.

3.

DAY 231

Jeremiah 26-29

NOTES AND REFLECTIONS

Study Notes

VERSE OF THE DAY JEREMIAH 29:13

PRAYER & PRAISE

TODAY I'M GRATEFUL FOR

1.

2.

3.

SEEKING  SCRIPTURE

NOTES AND REFLECTIONS

Study Notes

VERSE OF THE DAY JEREMIAH 31:33

PRAYER & PRAISE

TODAY I'M GRATEFUL FOR

1.

2.

3.

SEEKING  SCRIPTURE

DAY 233

Jeremiah 32-34

NOTES AND REFLECTIONS

Study Notes

VERSE OF THE DAY JEREMIAH 32:17

PRAYER & PRAISE

TODAY I'M GRATEFUL FOR

1.

2.

3.

SEEKING  SCRIPTURE

Jeremiah 35-37

NOTES AND REFLECTIONS

Study Notes

_____

_____

_____

_____

_____

_____

_____

_____

_____

_____

_____

VERSE OF THE DAY JEREMIAH 35:15

PRAYER & PRAISE

☀ ⛅ ☁ 🌧 ⛈ ❄
☐ ☐ ☐ ☐ ☐ ☐

TODAY I'M GRATEFUL FOR

1.

2.

3.

SEEKING  SCRIPTURE

DAY 235

Jeremiah 38-41

NOTES AND REFLECTIONS

Study Notes

VERSE OF THE DAY JEREMIAH 40:3

PRAYER & PRAISE

TODAY I'M GRATEFUL FOR

1.

2.

3.

DAY 236

NOTES AND REFLECTIONS

Jeremiah 42-45

Study Notes

VERSE OF THE DAY JEREMIAH 42:2

PRAYER & PRAISE

TODAY I'M GRATEFUL FOR

1.

2.

3.

SEEKING SCRIPTURE

DAY 237

Jeremiah 46-48

NOTES AND REFLECTIONS

Study Notes

_____

_____

_____

_____

_____

_____

_____

_____

_____

_____

_____

VERSE OF THE DAY JEREMIAH 46:27

TODAY I'M GRATEFUL FOR

1.

2.

3.

PRAYER & PRAISE

SEEKING  SCRIPTURE

NOTES AND REFLECTIONS

Study Notes

VERSE OF THE DAY JEREMIAH 50:5

PRAYER & PRAISE

TODAY I'M GRATEFUL FOR

1.

2.

3.

DAY 239

Jeremiah 51-52

NOTES AND REFLECTIONS

Study Notes

VERSE OF THE DAY JEREMIAH 51:5

PRAYER & PRAISE

TODAY I'M GRATEFUL FOR

1.

2.

3.

SEEKING  SCRIPTURE

NOTES AND REFLECTIONS

Study Notes

VERSE OF THE DAY LAMENTATIONS 3:21-23

PRAYER & PRAISE

TODAY I'M GRATEFUL FOR

1.

2.

3.

DAY 241

Lamentations 3:37-5

NOTES AND REFLECTIONS

Study Notes

_____
_____
_____
_____
_____
_____
_____
_____
_____
_____
_____
_____

VERSE OF THE DAY LAMENTATIONS 5:21

PRAYER & PRAISE

TODAY I'M GRATEFUL FOR

1.

2.

3.

SEEKING  SCRIPTURE

DAY 242

Ezekiel 1-4

NOTES AND REFLECTIONS

Study Notes

VERSE OF THE DAY EZEKIEL 2:7

PRAYER & PRAISE

TODAY I'M GRATEFUL FOR

1.

2.

3.

SEEKING  SCRIPTURE

DAY 243

Ezekiel 5-8

NOTES AND REFLECTIONS

Study Notes

VERSE OF THE DAY EZEKIEL 6:4

PRAYER & PRAISE

TODAY I'M GRATEFUL FOR

1.

2.

3.

SEEKING SCRIPTURE

NOTES AND REFLECTIONS

Ezekiel 9-12

Study Notes

_____
_____
_____
_____
_____
_____

_____
_____
_____
_____
_____
_____
_____

VERSE OF THE DAY EZEKIEL 11:12

PRAYER & PRAISE

TODAY I'M GRATEFUL FOR

1.

2.

3.

SEEKING  SCRIPTURE

DAY 245

Ezekiel 13-15

NOTES AND REFLECTIONS

Study Notes

VERSE OF THE DAY EZEKIEL 13:8

PRAYER & PRAISE

TODAY I'M GRATEFUL FOR

1.

2.

3.

SEEKING  SCRIPTURE

NOTES AND REFLECTIONS

Study Notes

VERSE OF THE DAY EZEKIEL 16:59

PRAYER & PRAISE

TODAY I'M GRATEFUL FOR

1.

2.

3.

SEEKING  SCRIPTURE

DAY 247

Ezekiel 18-20

Study Notes

NOTES AND REFLECTIONS

_____
_____
_____
_____
_____
_____
_____
_____
_____
_____
_____

VERSE OF THE DAY EZEKIEL 18:21

PRAYER & PRAISE

TODAY I'M GRATEFUL FOR

1.

2.

3.

SEEKING  SCRIPTURE

DAY 248
Ezekiel 21-22

NOTES AND REFLECTIONS

_____

_____

_____

_____

_____

Study Notes

_____

_____

_____

_____

_____

_____

_____

VERSE OF THE DAY EZEKIEL 22:30

PRAYER & PRAISE

☀ ⛅ ☁ 🌧 ⛈ ❄
☐ ☐ ☐ ☐ ☐ ☐

TODAY I'M GRATEFUL FOR

1.

2.

3.

255

SEEKING  SCRIPTURE

DAY 249

Ezekiel 23-24

Study Notes

VERSE OF THE DAY EZEKIEL 24:27

PRAYER & PRAISE

TODAY I'M GRATEFUL FOR

1.

2.

3.

SEEKING  SCRIPTURE

NOTES AND REFLECTIONS

_____
_____
_____
_____
_____
_____
_____
_____
_____
_____
_____
_____

Study Notes

VERSE OF THE DAY EZEKIEL 25:16

PRAYER & PRAISE

TODAY I'M GRATEFUL FOR

1.

2.

3.

SEEKING  SCRIPTURE

DAY 251

Ezekiel 28-30

Study Notes

NOTES AND REFLECTIONS

_____
_____
_____
_____
_____
_____
_____
_____
_____
_____
_____

VERSE OF THE DAY EZEKIEL 28:26

TODAY I'M GRATEFUL FOR

1.

2.

3.

PRAYER & PRAISE

SEEKING  SCRIPTURE

NOTES AND REFLECTIONS

_____
_____
_____
_____
_____

Study Notes

_____
_____
_____
_____
_____
_____

VERSE OF THE DAY EZEKIEL 33:7

PRAYER & PRAISE

TODAY I'M GRATEFUL FOR

1.

2.

3.

SEEKING  SCRIPTURE

DAY 253

Ezekiel 34-36

Study Notes

NOTES AND REFLECTIONS

_____
_____
_____
_____
_____
_____
_____
_____
_____
_____
_____
_____

VERSE OF THE DAY EZEKIEL 36:26

PRAYER & PRAISE

TODAY I'M GRATEFUL FOR

1.

2.

3.

SEEKING  SCRIPTURE

NOTES AND REFLECTIONS

Study Notes

VERSE OF THE DAY EZEKIEL 37:5

PRAYER & PRAISE

TODAY I'M GRATEFUL FOR

1.

2.

3.

SEEKING SCRIPTURE

DAY 255

Ezekiel 40-42

NOTES AND REFLECTIONS

Study Notes

VERSE OF THE DAY EZEKIEL 40:2

PRAYER & PRAISE

TODAY I'M GRATEFUL FOR

1.

2.

3.

SEEKING  SCRIPTURE

NOTES AND REFLECTIONS

Study Notes

VERSE OF THE DAY EZEKIEL 43:5

PRAYER & PRAISE

TODAY I'M GRATEFUL FOR

1.

2.

3.

SEEKING  SCRIPTURE

DAY 257

Ezekiel 46-48

NOTES AND REFLECTIONS

Study Notes

VERSE OF THE DAY EZEKIEL 46:1

PRAYER & PRAISE

TODAY I'M GRATEFUL FOR

1.

2.

3.

SEEKING  SCRIPTURE

Daniel 1-3

NOTES AND REFLECTIONS

_____
_____
_____
_____
_____

Study Notes

_____
_____
_____
_____
_____
_____
_____

VERSE OF THE DAY DANIEL 2:47

PRAYER & PRAISE

TODAY I'M GRATEFUL FOR

1.

2.

3.

SEEKING SCRIPTURE

DAY 259

Daniel 4-6

Study Notes

NOTES AND REFLECTIONS

_____
_____
_____
_____
_____
_____
_____
_____
_____
_____
_____

VERSE OF THE DAY DANIEL 4:3

TODAY I'M GRATEFUL FOR

1.

2.

3.

PRAYER & PRAISE

SEEKING  SCRIPTURE

NOTES AND REFLECTIONS

Daniel 7-9

Study Notes

VERSE OF THE DAY DANIEL 9:5

PRAYER & PRAISE

TODAY I'M GRATEFUL FOR

1.

2.

3.

SEEKING SCRIPTURE

Day 261

Daniel 10-12

Study Notes

VERSE OF THE DAY DANIEL 10:12

PRAYER & PRAISE

TODAY I'M GRATEFUL FOR

1.

2.

3.

SEEKING  SCRIPTURE

Hosea 1-7

NOTES AND REFLECTIONS

Study Notes

VERSE OF THE DAY HOSEA 6:1

PRAYER & PRAISE

TODAY I'M GRATEFUL FOR

1.

2.

3.

SEEKING SCRIPTURE

DAY 263

Hosea 8-14

Study Notes

VERSE OF THE DAY HOSEA 14:9

TODAY I'M GRATEFUL FOR

1.

2.

3.

PRAYER & PRAISE

SEEKING  SCRIPTURE

NOTES AND REFLECTIONS

Joel 1-3

Study Notes

_____
_____
_____
_____
_____
_____
_____
_____
_____
_____
_____
_____
_____

VERSE OF THE DAY JOEL 2:13

PRAYER & PRAISE

TODAY I'M GRATEFUL FOR

1.

2.

3.

SEEKING  SCRIPTURE

DAY 265

Amos 1-5

Study Notes

VERSE OF THE DAY AMOS 4:13

PRAYER & PRAISE

TODAY I'M GRATEFUL FOR

1.

2.

3.

SEEKING  SCRIPTURE

Amos 6-9

NOTES AND REFLECTIONS

Study Notes

VERSE OF THE DAY AMOS 8:11

PRAYER & PRAISE

TODAY I'M GRATEFUL FOR

1.

2.

3.

SEEKING  SCRIPTURE

DAY 267

Obadiah-Jonah

Study Notes

NOTES AND REFLECTIONS

VERSE OF THE DAY JONAH 2:8-9

TODAY I'M GRATEFUL FOR

1.

2.

3.

PRAYER & PRAISE

274

SEEKING SCRIPTURE

Micah 1-7

NOTES AND REFLECTIONS

Study Notes

VERSE OF THE DAY MICAH 4:2

PRAYER & PRAISE

TODAY I'M GRATEFUL FOR

1.

2.

3.

SEEKING  SCRIPTURE

DAY 269

Nahum 1-3

Study Notes

VERSE OF THE DAY NAHUM 1:7

PRAYER & PRAISE

TODAY I'M GRATEFUL FOR

1.

2.

3.

SEEKING  SCRIPTURE

NOTES AND REFLECTIONS

_____
_____
_____
_____
_____
_____

Study Notes

_____
_____
_____
_____
_____
_____

VERSE OF THE DAY HABAKKUK 2:4

PRAYER & PRAISE

TODAY I'M GRATEFUL FOR

1.

2.

3.

SEEKING SCRIPTURE

DAY 271

Haggai 1-2

Study Notes

NOTES AND REFLECTIONS

_____
_____
_____
_____
_____
_____
_____
_____
_____
_____
_____
_____

VERSE OF THE DAY HAGGAI 2:9

TODAY I'M GRATEFUL FOR

1.

2.

3.

PRAYER & PRAISE

NOTES AND REFLECTIONS

Study Notes

VERSE OF THE DAY ZECHARIAH 1:16

PRAYER & PRAISE

TODAY I'M GRATEFUL FOR

1.

2.

3.

SEEKING  SCRIPTURE

DAY 273

Zechariah 8-14

NOTES AND REFLECTIONS

Study Notes

_____

VERSE OF THE DAY ZECHARIAH 8:15

PRAYER & PRAISE

TODAY I'M GRATEFUL FOR

1.

2.

3.

SEEKING  SCRIPTURE

NOTES AND REFLECTIONS

Malachi 1-4

Study Notes

_____

_____

_____

_____

_____

_____

_____

_____

_____

_____

_____

VERSE OF THE DAY MALACHI 3:6

PRAYER & PRAISE

TODAY I'M GRATEFUL FOR

1.

2.

3.

SEEKING  SCRIPTURE

DAY 275

Matthew 1-4

NOTES AND REFLECTIONS

Study Notes

_____

VERSE OF THE DAY MATTHEW 3:2

PRAYER & PRAISE

TODAY I'M GRATEFUL FOR

1.

2.

3.

SEEKING  SCRIPTURE

NOTES AND REFLECTIONS

Study Notes

VERSE OF THE DAY MATTHEW 5:17–18

PRAYER & PRAISE

TODAY I'M GRATEFUL FOR

1.

2.

3.

SEEKING  SCRIPTURE

DAY 277

Matthew 7-8

NOTES AND REFLECTIONS

Study Notes

VERSE OF THE DAY MATTHEW 7:2

PRAYER & PRAISE

TODAY I'M GRATEFUL FOR

1.

2.

3.

SEEKING  SCRIPTURE

NOTES AND REFLECTIONS

Study Notes

VERSE OF THE DAY MATTHEW 9:13

PRAYER & PRAISE

TODAY I'M GRATEFUL FOR

1.

2.

3.

SEEKING  SCRIPTURE

DAY 279

Matthew 11-12

NOTES AND REFLECTIONS

Study Notes

_____

VERSE OF THE DAY MATTHEW 12:36

PRAYER & PRAISE

TODAY I'M GRATEFUL FOR

1.

2.

3.

SEEKING  SCRIPTURE

NOTES AND REFLECTIONS

Study Notes

VERSE OF THE DAY MATTHEW 14:31

PRAYER & PRAISE

TODAY I'M GRATEFUL FOR

1.

2.

3.

SEEKING  SCRIPTURE

DAY 281

Matthew 15-17

Study Notes

NOTES AND REFLECTIONS

_____
_____
_____
_____
_____
_____
_____
_____
_____
_____
_____
_____

VERSE OF THE DAY MATTHEW 15:8-9

TODAY I'M GRATEFUL FOR

1.

2.

3.

PRAYER & PRAISE

SEEKING  SCRIPTURE

NOTES AND REFLECTIONS

Study Notes

VERSE OF THE DAY MATTHEW 19:17

PRAYER & PRAISE

TODAY I'M GRATEFUL FOR

1.

2.

3.

SEEKING SCRIPTURE

DAY 283

Matthew 20-21

Study Notes

VERSE OF THE DAY MATTHEW 20:28

PRAYER & PRAISE

TODAY I'M GRATEFUL FOR

1.

2.

3.

SEEKING  SCRIPTURE

NOTES AND REFLECTIONS

Study Notes

VERSE OF THE DAY MATTHEW 23:39

PRAYER & PRAISE

TODAY I'M GRATEFUL FOR

1.

2.

3.

SEEKING SCRIPTURE

DAY 285

Matthew 24-25

NOTES AND REFLECTIONS

Study Notes

_____
_____
_____
_____
_____
_____
_____
_____
_____
_____
_____

VERSE OF THE DAY MATTHEW 24:4-5

PRAYER & PRAISE

TODAY I'M GRATEFUL FOR

1.

2.

3.

SEEKING  SCRIPTURE

DAY 286
Matthew 26

NOTES AND REFLECTIONS

Study Notes

VERSE OF THE DAY MATTHEW 26:10-11

PRAYER & PRAISE

TODAY I'M GRATEFUL FOR

1.

2.

3.

DAY 287

Matthew 27-28

NOTES AND REFLECTIONS

Study Notes

VERSE OF THE DAY MATTHEW 27:51-52

PRAYER & PRAISE

TODAY I'M GRATEFUL FOR

1.

2.

3.

SEEKING  SCRIPTURE

NOTES AND REFLECTIONS

_____
_____
_____
_____
_____

Study Notes

_____
_____
_____
_____
_____
_____
_____

VERSE OF THE DAY MARK 2:8

PRAYER & PRAISE

TODAY I'M GRATEFUL FOR

1.

2.

3.

SEEKING SCRIPTURE

DAY 289

Mark 4-5

Study Notes

VERSE OF THE DAY MARK 4:11

PRAYER & PRAISE

TODAY I'M GRATEFUL FOR

1.

2.

3.

SEEKING  SCRIPTURE

NOTES AND REFLECTIONS

_____

_____

_____

_____

_____

Study Notes

_____

_____

_____

_____

_____

_____

VERSE OF THE DAY MARK 6:50

PRAYER & PRAISE

TODAY I'M GRATEFUL FOR

1.

2.

3.

SEEKING SCRIPTURE

DAY 291

Mark 8-9

NOTES AND REFLECTIONS

Study Notes

VERSE OF THE DAY MARK 8:36

PRAYER & PRAISE

TODAY I'M GRATEFUL FOR

1.

2.

3.

SEEKING  SCRIPTURE

NOTES AND REFLECTIONS

Study Notes

VERSE OF THE DAY MARK 10:15-16

PRAYER & PRAISE

TODAY I'M GRATEFUL FOR

1.

2.

3.

SEEKING SCRIPTURE

DAY 293

Mark 12-13

Study Notes

_____
_____
_____
_____
_____
_____
_____
_____
_____
_____
_____

VERSE OF THE DAY MARK 12:24

PRAYER & PRAISE

TODAY I'M GRATEFUL FOR

1.

2.

3.

SEEKING SCRIPTURE

NOTES AND REFLECTIONS

_____
_____
_____
_____
_____
_____

Study Notes

_____
_____
_____
_____
_____
_____

VERSE OF THE DAY MARK 14:62

PRAYER & PRAISE

TODAY I'M GRATEFUL FOR

1.

2.

3.

SEEKING SCRIPTURE

DAY 295

Mark 15-16

NOTES AND REFLECTIONS

Study Notes

VERSE OF THE DAY MARK 16:6

PRAYER & PRAISE

TODAY I'M GRATEFUL FOR

1.

2.

3.

SEEKING  SCRIPTURE

Luke 1

NOTES AND REFLECTIONS

Study Notes

VERSE OF THE DAY LUKE 1:76-77

PRAYER & PRAISE

TODAY I'M GRATEFUL FOR

1.

2.

3.

SEEKING SCRIPTURE

DAY 297

Luke 2-3

NOTES AND REFLECTIONS

Study Notes

VERSE OF THE DAY LUKE 2:11

PRAYER & PRAISE

TODAY I'M GRATEFUL FOR

1.

2.

3.

SEEKING  SCRIPTURE

Luke 4-5

NOTES AND REFLECTIONS

Study Notes

VERSE OF THE DAY LUKE 4:43

PRAYER & PRAISE

TODAY I'M GRATEFUL FOR

1.

2.

3.

SEEKING SCRIPTURE

DAY 299

Luke 6-7

Study Notes

_____

VERSE OF THE DAY LUKE 6:35

PRAYER & PRAISE

TODAY I'M GRATEFUL FOR

1.

2.

3.

SEEKING  SCRIPTURE

NOTES AND REFLECTIONS

Study Notes

VERSE OF THE DAY LUKE 8:21

PRAYER & PRAISE

TODAY I'M GRATEFUL FOR

1.

2.

3.

SEEKING SCRIPTURE

DAY 301

Luke 10-11

Study Notes

VERSE OF THE DAY LUKE 11:28

PRAYER & PRAISE

TODAY I'M GRATEFUL FOR

1.

2.

3.

SEEKING SCRIPTURE

NOTES AND REFLECTIONS

Study Notes

VERSE OF THE DAY LUKE 12:7

PRAYER & PRAISE

TODAY I'M GRATEFUL FOR

1.

2.

3.

SEEKING SCRIPTURE

DAY 303

Luke 14-16

Study Notes

VERSE OF THE DAY LUKE 15:7

PRAYER & PRAISE

TODAY I'M GRATEFUL FOR

1.

2.

3.

SEEKING  SCRIPTURE

NOTES AND REFLECTIONS

_____

_____

_____

_____

_____

Study Notes

_____

_____

_____

_____

_____

_____

VERSE OF THE DAY LUKE 17:15

PRAYER & PRAISE

TODAY I'M GRATEFUL FOR

1.

2.

3.

SEEKING SCRIPTURE

DAY 305

Luke 19-20

NOTES AND REFLECTIONS

Study Notes

VERSE OF THE DAY LUKE 20:25

PRAYER & PRAISE

TODAY I'M GRATEFUL FOR

1.

2.

3.

SEEKING SCRIPTURE

NOTES AND REFLECTIONS

Study Notes

VERSE OF THE DAY LUKE 21:33

PRAYER & PRAISE

TODAY I'M GRATEFUL FOR

1.

2.

3.

SEEKING SCRIPTURE

DAY 307

Luke 23-24

NOTES AND REFLECTIONS

Study Notes

_____

VERSE OF THE DAY LUKE 24:44

PRAYER & PRAISE

TODAY I'M GRATEFUL FOR

1.

2.

3.

SEEKING  SCRIPTURE

NOTES AND REFLECTIONS

Study Notes

VERSE OF THE DAY JOHN 1:14

PRAYER & PRAISE

TODAY I'M GRATEFUL FOR

1.

2.

3.

SEEKING  SCRIPTURE

DAY 309

John 3-4

NOTES AND REFLECTIONS

Study Notes

VERSE OF THE DAY JOHN 3:30

PRAYER & PRAISE

TODAY I'M GRATEFUL FOR

1.

2.

3.

SEEKING SCRIPTURE

NOTES AND REFLECTIONS

Study Notes

VERSE OF THE DAY JOHN 5:46-47

PRAYER & PRAISE

TODAY I'M GRATEFUL FOR

1.

2.

3.

SEEKING SCRIPTURE

DAY 311

John 7-8

NOTES AND REFLECTIONS

Study Notes

_____

VERSE OF THE DAY JOHN 8:28

PRAYER & PRAISE

TODAY I'M GRATEFUL FOR

1.

2.

3.

SEEKING SCRIPTURE

NOTES AND REFLECTIONS

Study Notes

VERSE OF THE DAY JOHN 10:9

PRAYER & PRAISE

TODAY I'M GRATEFUL FOR

1.

2.

3.

SEEKING SCRIPTURE

DAY 313

John 11-12

Study Notes

NOTES AND REFLECTIONS

_____
_____
_____
_____
_____
_____
_____
_____
_____
_____
_____
_____

VERSE OF THE DAY JOHN 12:42

TODAY I'M GRATEFUL FOR

1.

2.

3.

PRAYER & PRAISE

SEEKING SCRIPTURE

NOTES AND REFLECTIONS

Study Notes

VERSE OF THE DAY JOHN 14:21

PRAYER & PRAISE

TODAY I'M GRATEFUL FOR

1.

2.

3.

SEEKING SCRIPTURE

DAY 315

John 16-18

Study Notes

VERSE OF THE DAY JOHN 16:33

PRAYER & PRAISE

TODAY I'M GRATEFUL FOR

1.

2.

3.

SEEKING  SCRIPTURE

NOTES AND REFLECTIONS

Study Notes

VERSE OF THE DAY JOHN 20:29

PRAYER & PRAISE

TODAY I'M GRATEFUL FOR

1.

2.

3.

SEEKING SCRIPTURE

DAY 317

Acts 1-3

Study Notes

NOTES AND REFLECTIONS

VERSE OF THE DAY ACTS 2:42

PRAYER & PRAISE

TODAY I'M GRATEFUL FOR

1.

2.

3.

SEEKING  SCRIPTURE

DAY 318

Acts 4-6

NOTES AND REFLECTIONS

_____
_____
_____
_____
_____

Study Notes

_____
_____
_____
_____
_____

VERSE OF THE DAY ACTS 5:29

PRAYER & PRAISE

TODAY I'M GRATEFUL FOR

1.

2.

3.

325

SEEKING SCRIPTURE

DAY 319

Acts 7-8

NOTES AND REFLECTIONS

Study Notes

VERSE OF THE DAY ACTS 7:56

PRAYER & PRAISE

TODAY I'M GRATEFUL FOR

1.

2.

3.

SEEKING  SCRIPTURE

Acts 9-10

NOTES AND REFLECTIONS

_____

_____

_____

_____

_____

_____

_____

_____

_____

_____

_____

_____

_____

Study Notes

VERSE OF THE DAY ACTS 10:34-35

PRAYER & PRAISE

TODAY I'M GRATEFUL FOR

1.

2.

3.

SEEKING  SCRIPTURE

DAY 321

Acts 11-13

NOTES AND REFLECTIONS

Study Notes

VERSE OF THE DAY ACTS 13:52

PRAYER & PRAISE

TODAY I'M GRATEFUL FOR

1.

2.

3.

SEEKING  SCRIPTURE

NOTES AND REFLECTIONS

_____
_____
_____
_____
_____

Study Notes

_____
_____
_____
_____
_____
_____

VERSE OF THE DAY ACTS 15:32

PRAYER & PRAISE

TODAY I'M GRATEFUL FOR

1.

2.

3.

SEEKING SCRIPTURE

DAY 323

Acts 16-17

Study Notes

NOTES AND REFLECTIONS

_____

_____

_____

_____

_____

_____

_____

_____

_____

_____

_____

VERSE OF THE DAY ACTS 17:11

PRAYER & PRAISE

TODAY I'M GRATEFUL FOR

1.

2.

3.

SEEKING  SCRIPTURE

DAY 324

Acts 18-20

NOTES AND REFLECTIONS

Study Notes

VERSE OF THE DAY ACTS 19:20

PRAYER & PRAISE

☀ ⛅ ☁ 🌧 ⛈ ❄
☐ ☐ ☐ ☐ ☐ ☐

TODAY I'M GRATEFUL FOR

1.

2.

3.

SEEKING ✦ SCRIPTURE

DAY 325

Acts 21-23

NOTES AND REFLECTIONS

Study Notes

_____

_____

_____

_____

_____

_____

_____

_____

_____

_____

_____

VERSE OF THE DAY ACTS 21:13

TODAY I'M GRATEFUL FOR

1.

2.

3.

PRAYER & PRAISE

SEEKING SCRIPTURE

NOTES AND REFLECTIONS

Study Notes

VERSE OF THE DAY ACTS 24:14

PRAYER & PRAISE

TODAY I'M GRATEFUL FOR

1.

2.

3.

SEEKING SCRIPTURE

DAY 327

Acts 27-28

Study Notes

NOTES AND REFLECTIONS

_____
_____
_____
_____
_____
_____
_____
_____
_____
_____
_____
_____

VERSE OF THE DAY ACTS 28:28

TODAY I'M GRATEFUL FOR

1.

2.

3.

PRAYER & PRAISE

SEEKING  SCRIPTURE

NOTES AND REFLECTIONS

_____

_____

_____

_____

_____

_____

_____

_____

_____

_____

_____

_____

Study Notes

VERSE OF THE DAY ROMANS 1:16

PRAYER & PRAISE

TODAY I'M GRATEFUL FOR

1.

2.

3.

SEEKING SCRIPTURE

DAY 329

Romans 4-7

Study Notes

NOTES AND REFLECTIONS

_____
_____
_____
_____
_____
_____
_____
_____
_____
_____
_____
_____
_____

VERSE OF THE DAY ROMANS 6:1-2

PRAYER & PRAISE

TODAY I'M GRATEFUL FOR

1.

2.

3.

SEEKING  SCRIPTURE

DAY 330

Romans 8-10

NOTES AND REFLECTIONS

Study Notes

VERSE OF THE DAY ROMANS 8:7-8

PRAYER & PRAISE

TODAY I'M GRATEFUL FOR

1.

2.

3.

337

SEEKING  SCRIPTURE

DAY 331

Romans 11-13

NOTES AND REFLECTIONS

Study Notes

_____

VERSE OF THE DAY ROMANS 12:3

PRAYER & PRAISE

TODAY I'M GRATEFUL FOR

1.

2.

3.

SEEKING  SCRIPTURE

NOTES AND REFLECTIONS

Study Notes

VERSE OF THE DAY ROMANS 14:4

PRAYER & PRAISE

TODAY I'M GRATEFUL FOR

1.

2.

3.

SEEKING  SCRIPTURE

DAY 333

1 Corinthians 1-4

NOTES AND REFLECTIONS

Study Notes

_____

VERSE OF THE DAY 1 CORINTHIANS 2:12

PRAYER & PRAISE

TODAY I'M GRATEFUL FOR

1.

2.

3.

340

SEEKING ✺ SCRIPTURE

1.

NOTES AND REFLECTIONS

1 Corinthians 5-8

Study Notes

_____
_____
_____
_____
_____
_____
_____
_____
_____
_____
_____

VERSE OF THE DAY 1 CORINTHIANS 8:6

PRAYER & PRAISE

TODAY I'M GRATEFUL FOR

1.

2.

3.

SEEKING SCRIPTURE

DAY 335
1 Corinthians 9-11

Study Notes

_____
_____
_____
_____
_____

_____
_____
_____
_____
_____
_____
_____

VERSE OF THE DAY 1 CORINTHIANS 10:13

PRAYER & PRAISE

TODAY I'M GRATEFUL FOR

1.

2.

3.

SEEKING  SCRIPTURE

NOTES AND REFLECTIONS

Study Notes

VERSE OF THE DAY 1 CORINTHIANS 12:26-27

PRAYER & PRAISE

TODAY I'M GRATEFUL FOR

1.

2.

3.

SEEKING SCRIPTURE

DAY 337

1 Corinthians 15-16

Study Notes

VERSE OF THE DAY 1 CORINTHIANS 15:33-34

PRAYER & PRAISE

TODAY I'M GRATEFUL FOR

1.

2.

3.

SEEKING  SCRIPTURE

NOTES AND REFLECTIONS

Study Notes

VERSE OF THE DAY 2 CORINTHIANS 4:6

PRAYER & PRAISE

TODAY I'M GRATEFUL FOR

1.

2.

3.

SEEKING SCRIPTURE

DAY 339

2 Corinthians 5-9

Study Notes

VERSE OF THE DAY 2 CORINTHIANS 6:17-18

PRAYER & PRAISE

TODAY I'M GRATEFUL FOR

1.

2.

3.

SEEKING  SCRIPTURE

DAY 340

2 Corinthians 10-13

NOTES AND REFLECTIONS

Study Notes

VERSE OF THE DAY 2 CORINTHIANS 13:5

PRAYER & PRAISE

TODAY I'M GRATEFUL FOR

1.

2.

3.

SEEKING SCRIPTURE

DAY 341

Galatians 1-3

Study Notes

_____

VERSE OF THE DAY GALATIANS 2:20

PRAYER & PRAISE

TODAY I'M GRATEFUL FOR

1.

2.

3.

SEEKING  SCRIPTURE

NOTES AND REFLECTIONS

Galatians 4-6

Study Notes

VERSE OF THE DAY GALATIANS 5:7

PRAYER & PRAISE

TODAY I'M GRATEFUL FOR

1.

2.

3.

SEEKING SCRIPTURE

DAY 343

Ephesians 1-3

Study Notes

NOTES AND REFLECTIONS

_____
_____
_____
_____
_____
_____
_____
_____
_____
_____
_____
_____

VERSE OF THE DAY EPHESIANS 2:8

PRAYER & PRAISE

TODAY I'M GRATEFUL FOR

1.

2.

3.

SEEKING  SCRIPTURE

NOTES AND REFLECTIONS

Ephesians 4-6

_____
_____
_____
_____
_____

Study Notes

_____
_____
_____
_____
_____
_____
_____

VERSE OF THE DAY EPHESIANS 4:32

PRAYER & PRAISE

☀ ⛅ ☁ 🌧 ⛈ ❄
☐ ☐ ☐ ☐ ☐ ☐

TODAY I'M GRATEFUL FOR

1.

2.

3.

SEEKING  SCRIPTURE

DAY 345

Philippians 1-4

NOTES AND REFLECTIONS

Study Notes

_____
_____
_____
_____
_____

_____
_____
_____
_____
_____
_____
_____

VERSE OF THE DAY PHILIPPIANS 2:12

PRAYER & PRAISE

TODAY I'M GRATEFUL FOR

1.

2.

3.

SEEKING  SCRIPTURE

NOTES AND REFLECTIONS

_____
_____
_____
_____
_____
_____
_____
_____
_____
_____
_____
_____

Study Notes

VERSE OF THE DAY COLOSSIANS 3:17

PRAYER & PRAISE

TODAY I'M GRATEFUL FOR

1.

2.

3.

SEEKING SCRIPTURE

DAY 347

1 Thessalonians 1-5

NOTES AND REFLECTIONS

Study Notes

VERSE OF THE DAY 1 THESSALONIANS 3:12

PRAYER & PRAISE

TODAY I'M GRATEFUL FOR

1.

2.

3.

SEEKING  SCRIPTURE

NOTES AND REFLECTIONS

2 Thessalonians 1-3

Study Notes

VERSE OF THE DAY 2 THESSALONIANS 1:11

PRAYER & PRAISE

TODAY I'M GRATEFUL FOR

1.

2.

3.

SEEKING SCRIPTURE

DAY 349
1 Timothy 1-6

Study Notes

VERSE OF THE DAY 1 TIMOTHY 4:7-8

PRAYER & PRAISE

TODAY I'M GRATEFUL FOR

1.

2.

3.

SEEKING  SCRIPTURE

NOTES AND REFLECTIONS

_____
_____
_____
_____
_____

Study Notes

_____
_____
_____
_____
_____

VERSE OF THE DAY 2 TIMOTHY 1:14

PRAYER & PRAISE

TODAY I'M GRATEFUL FOR

1.

2.

3.

SEEKING SCRIPTURE

DAY 351

Titus-Philemon

Study Notes

NOTES AND REFLECTIONS

_____
_____
_____
_____
_____
_____
_____
_____
_____
_____
_____
_____

VERSE OF THE DAY TITUS 2:7–8

TODAY I'M GRATEFUL FOR

1.

2.

3.

PRAYER & PRAISE

SEEKING  SCRIPTURE

NOTES AND REFLECTIONS

Study Notes

VERSE OF THE DAY HEBREWS 2:1

PRAYER & PRAISE

TODAY I'M GRATEFUL FOR

1.

2.

3.

SEEKING SCRIPTURE

DAY 353

Hebrews 7-10

Study Notes

NOTES AND REFLECTIONS

_____

VERSE OF THE DAY HEBREWS 7:26

PRAYER & PRAISE

TODAY I'M GRATEFUL FOR

1.

2.

3.

SEEKING  SCRIPTURE

NOTES AND REFLECTIONS

_____
_____
_____
_____
_____

Study Notes

_____
_____
_____
_____
_____
_____

VERSE OF THE DAY HEBREWS 12:1-2

PRAYER & PRAISE

TODAY I'M GRATEFUL FOR

1.

2.

3.

SEEKING SCRIPTURE

DAY 355

James 1-5

NOTES AND REFLECTIONS

Study Notes

VERSE OF THE DAY JAMES 2:18

PRAYER & PRAISE

TODAY I'M GRATEFUL FOR

1.

2.

3.

SEEKING  SCRIPTURE

NOTES AND REFLECTIONS

Study Notes

VERSE OF THE DAY 1 PETER 1:14-16

PRAYER & PRAISE

TODAY I'M GRATEFUL FOR

1.

2.

3.

SEEKING SCRIPTURE

DAY 357

2 Peter 1-3

Study Notes

_____
_____
_____
_____
_____
_____
_____
_____
_____
_____
_____
_____

VERSE OF THE DAY 2 PETER 3:9

PRAYER & PRAISE

TODAY I'M GRATEFUL FOR

1.

2.

3.

SEEKING  SCRIPTURE

DAY 358

1 John 1-5

NOTES AND REFLECTIONS

_____
_____
_____
_____
_____

Study Notes

_____
_____
_____
_____
_____
_____

VERSE OF THE DAY 1 JOHN 2:3-4

PRAYER & PRAISE

TODAY I'M GRATEFUL FOR

1.

2.

3.

SEEKING SCRIPTURE

DAY 359

2 John-Jude

NOTES AND REFLECTIONS

Study Notes

VERSE OF THE DAY 2 JOHN 1:6

PRAYER & PRAISE

TODAY I'M GRATEFUL FOR

1.

2.

3.

SEEKING  SCRIPTURE

NOTES AND REFLECTIONS

Revelation 1-3

Study Notes

_____

_____

_____

_____

_____

_____

_____

_____

_____

_____

_____

VERSE OF THE DAY REVELATION 1:8

PRAYER & PRAISE

TODAY I'M GRATEFUL FOR

1.

2.

3.

SEEKING SCRIPTURE

DAY 361

Revelation 4-8

Study Notes

NOTES AND REFLECTIONS

_____
_____
_____
_____
_____

_____
_____
_____
_____
_____
_____

VERSE OF THE DAY REVELATION 4:2

PRAYER & PRAISE

TODAY I'M GRATEFUL FOR

1.

2.

3.

SEEKING  SCRIPTURE

Revelation 9-12

NOTES AND REFLECTIONS

Study Notes

VERSE OF THE DAY REVELATION 11:3

PRAYER & PRAISE

TODAY I'M GRATEFUL FOR

1.

2.

3.

SEEKING SCRIPTURE

DAY 363

Revelation 13-16

Study Notes

NOTES AND REFLECTIONS

_____
_____
_____
_____
_____
_____
_____
_____
_____
_____
_____

VERSE OF THE DAY REVELATION 14:1

PRAYER & PRAISE

TODAY I'M GRATEFUL FOR

1.

2.

3.

SEEKING  SCRIPTURE

NOTES AND REFLECTIONS

Revelation 17-19

Study Notes

VERSE OF THE DAY REVELATION 19:6

PRAYER & PRAISE

TODAY I'M GRATEFUL FOR

1.

2.

3.

SEEKING SCRIPTURE

DAY 365

Revelation 20-22

NOTES AND REFLECTIONS

_____
_____
_____
_____

Study Notes

_____

_____
_____
_____
_____
_____
_____
_____

VERSE OF THE DAY REVELATION 22:3

PRAYER & PRAISE

TODAY I'M GRATEFUL FOR

1.

2.

3.

To MaryAnne,
You brought forth strength from weakness,
joy from sadness, and hope from despair.
I look forward to hearing your laughter again.
You are so missed.

SEEKING
Scripture

Visit us online
SeekingScripture.com

Read our Charter &
Statement of Purpose

Request to join our Discussion Group*

*We only admit new members to our Facebook discussion group during the month of December, just before the new reading cycle starts. We reccommend requesting to join as soon as possible.

SEEKING  SCRIPTURE

Bible Reading Checklist

Track your progress

- [ ] Genesis
- [ ] Exodus
- [ ] Leviticus
- [ ] Numbers
- [ ] Deuteronomy
- [ ] Joshua
- [ ] Judges
- [ ] Ruth
- [ ] 1 Samuel
- [ ] 2 Samuel
- [ ] 1 Kings
- [ ] 2 Kings
- [ ] 1 Chronicles
- [ ] 2 Chronicles
- [ ] Ezra
- [ ] Nehemiah
- [ ] Esther
- [ ] Job
- [ ] Psalms
- [ ] Proverbs
- [ ] Ecclesiastes
- [ ] Song of Solomon
- [ ] Isaiah
- [ ] Jeremiah
- [ ] Lamentations

- [ ] Ezekiel
- [ ] Daniel
- [ ] Hosea
- [ ] Joel
- [ ] Amos
- [ ] Obadiah
- [ ] Jonah
- [ ] Micah
- [ ] Nahum
- [ ] Habakkuk
- [ ] Zephaniah
- [ ] Haggai
- [ ] Zechariah
- [ ] Malachi
- [ ] Matthew
- [ ] Mark
- [ ] Luke
- [ ] John
- [ ] Acts
- [ ] Romans
- [ ] 1 Corinthians
- [ ] 2 Corinthians
- [ ] Galatians
- [ ] Ephesians
- [ ] Philippians

- [ ] Colossians
- [ ] 1 Thessalonians
- [ ] 2 Thessalonians
- [ ] 1 Timothy
- [ ] 2 Timothy
- [ ] Titus
- [ ] Philemon
- [ ] Hebrews
- [ ] James
- [ ] 1 Peter
- [ ] 2 Peter
- [ ] 1 John
- [ ] 2 John
- [ ] 3 John
- [ ] Jude
- [ ] Revelation

Made in the USA
Middletown, DE
22 November 2024